The Pronunciation of English: A Workbook

The Pronunciation of English: A Workbook

Joanne Kenworthy

Senior Lecturer in Linguistics
University of East London

ARNOLD

A member of the Hodder Headline Group
LONDON

Co-published in the United States of America by
Oxford University Press Inc., New York

First published in Great Britain in 2000 by
Arnold, a member of the Hodder Headline Group,
338 Euston Road, London NW1 3BH

http://www.arnoldpublishers.com

Co-published in the United States of America by
Oxford University Press Inc.,
198 Madison Avenue, New York, NY10016

British Library Cataloguing in Publication Data
A catalogue record for this book is available from the British Library

Library of Congress Cataloging-in-Publication Data
A catalog record for this book is available from the Library of Congress

ISBN 0 340 73123 0

1 2 3 4 5 6 7 8 9 10

Production Editor: Julie Delf
Production Controller: Priya Gohil
Cover design: Mouse Mat Design

Typeset in 10.5 on 12.5 pt Times by Cambrian Typesetters, Frimley, Surrey
Printed and bound in Great Britain by J. W. Arrowsmith Ltd, Bristol

What do you think about this book? Or any other Arnold title?
Please send your comments to feedback.arnold@hodder.co.uk

Contents

Introduction

At the centre of each of the units in this workbook is a recording from which a set of extracts, referred to as 'sequences', have been selected. For each of these sequences, there are various exercises, tasks and questions which constitute the 'work' of this workbook. These have been designed in order to present, illustrate, and analyse particular features of the pronunciation of English.

Each unit has the following structure:

1 A section called 'Preview', which identifies the particular aspects of pronunciation that will be the focus of the exercises.
2 A 'Background' section gives information about the person or people you will hear, their relationship, what they were talking about, where they were recorded, why they were talking, and what kind of setting or speaking situation they were in. There may also be some points of information that will help you understand the content of what they were saying.
3 The exercises and tasks based on the extracts.
4 A section called 'Looking Back', which gives a summary of what has been covered and a reminder of the key points.
5 The final section is called 'Tasks for Extension or Discussion'. If you are working in a group, then these are some suggestions for group discussion, or for activities that you could do together. If you are working by yourself, you could use these ideas for exploring or thinking about the points covered in the units in more detail.

Each unit has another section – the 'Key and Comments'. After you attempt each exercise or question, the Key symbol ![key] will refer you to this section, where you will find suggested answers. Also included here are notes and points about important issues and concepts, hence the heading 'Key and Comments'. Some of these issues are theoretical. The way we describe and analyse spoken language is inevitably based on our mental model of what spoken language is. This workbook is not designed to address these issues in any detail, so references will be given in a 'Further reading and references' section for those who want to explore these.

In organizing the workbook in this way, the intention is that users attempt an exercise or question and then consult the 'Key and Comments' before going onto the next one. But in some cases, you may want to work through all the exercises in a unit or section of a unit and then consult the 'Key and Comments' section.

Each unit is designed to be complete in itself. There are cross-references to other units, but these have generally been kept to a minimum. This means that it is possible to select particular units, instead of working through them all in order. It is to be hoped that this will make the workbook quite flexible and adaptable for many different purposes.

However, Units 1, 2, 4 and 5 worked through in order should give you an overview of the basic areas of pronunciation. Units 3 and 6–12 consolidate these areas, extend and develop certain aspects and issues, and provide more opportunities for practice and analysis. But this does not mean that the book falls into two parts. Its structure can be described as cyclical. Although an area such as intonation ('speech melody') is first presented in Unit 4, there are many exercises on the intonation patterns used by speakers in other units, and in these, basic points will be returned to and further dimensions investigated.

In order to help you if you want to work on particular aspects of the pronunciation of English, a 'Subject Reference Guide', listing the areas treated in each unit, is provided after this Introduction.

The aim of this workbook is to provide a complement or a companion to the study of English pronunciation. It is designed to be linked to other types of work – class discussion, reading, private study, revision and consolidation of class work, and so on.

Throughout the book there are references to the fifth edition of A. C. Gimson's *Pronunciation of English* revised by Alan Cruttenden. These references are shown by the abbreviation 'PE5' and the relevant chapter, section number, or page of the book. Users can therefore consult these parts of this classic description of phonetics and spoken English if they wish.

This workbook has been organized with recordings of real speech at its core in order to put the spotlight on the raw material of the study of the pronunciation of English – the voices of people speaking English to real listeners in real situations. Its overall aim is to give users the opportunity to listen, to listen *carefully*, to become aware of the choices speakers make as they speak.

The recordings are the starting point for analysis and discussion. But the exercises that have been designed for the recording in each unit are certainly not exhaustive, and, indeed, at times are very selective. This means that the recordings themselves can be treated as a resource for anyone using this book. Further practice activities can be added, and the recordings can be exploited in a variety of ways.

English is spoken by many millions of people in the world today. Because of this, the voices you will hear represent a range of the accents and varieties of

English, and even a sample of how linguists think the language sounded in the past. They also represent a range of speakers in terms of age – from a child aged two and a half years to a man and a woman both in their seventies – and background, ranging from a poet to a doctor to a woman who has spent all of her life in the small villages of Cornwall. Some of the recordings were made in a studio, some were made in people's homes or their place of work, or at venues such as a conference or a church service. All the speakers were using English for the purposes and reasons that they usually do, and talking about the things they are interested in and that concern them.

However, within all this variety we find the constant or essential features and processes of spoken English. This is the purpose of this workbook – to help you understand how the 'sound of English' is produced and how speakers use it.

Subject reference guide to the units

Unit 3

high (or close) rounded front vowel /y/
alveolar trill
transcription practice
variation of sounds in different environments

Unit 4

pitch movement
falling and rising tones
rise-fall and fall-rise
pitch range
level tones

Unit 5

rhythm
stressed and unstressed syllables
the foot
analysis of metre
silent stress

Unit 6

word stress patterns in complex words
accent-neutral suffixes
accent-attracting suffixes
word stress patterns in compound words
secondary stress
weak forms of 'can', 'do', 'to'
practice in transcribing intonation
use of pauses
glottal stop

Unit 7

tone units (or groups)
intonation and information structure
deletion of initial /h/
rhotic and non-rhotic pronunciations
/tr-/ and /dr-/ as affricates
affricated plosives
examples of speech simplifications

Unit 8

linking r
use of /j/ in English words, e.g. 'tube'
/w/ and /h/ pronunciations in words, e.g. 'weather'/'whether'
variation in the pronunciation of 'the' and 'to'
practice in hearing stressed syllables
practice in transcribing intonation

Unit 9

analysis of the pronunciation of a speaker of English as an additional language
(first language: Brazilian Portuguese)
analysis of vowel/consonants
word stress patterns
syllable structure patterns

Unit 10

the use of paralinguistic features
analysis of pronunciation of three speakers of English as an additional language
(first languages: Japanese, Italian, Spanish)

Unit 11

analysis of the use of intonation by speakers talking about their experiences to
one or more listeners

Unit 12

analysis of the pronunciation of a three and a half year old child
homorganic consonants/clusters
nasal plosion
syllabic n
lateral plosion
syllabic l
intonation patterns in interaction

List of symbols and transcript conventions

The symbols used in this book are those devised by the International Phonetics Association. The full set of symbols is given at the end of this section.

Below is a list of the consonant phonemes of English with example words for each:

p   pen support hip
b   bed above cub
t   tea attach let
d   day leader lad
k   keep account rock
g   give again bag
tʃ   check nature patch
dʒ   joke age soldier
f   fact coffee cough
v   value heavy move
θ   thing author both
ð   these other smooth
s   sun sister peace
z   zone roses buzz
ʃ   sure station bush
ʒ   pleasure vision
h   hat behind
m   move summer hum
n   now funny son
ŋ   ring
l   lip valley feel
r   right sorry
j   yet use
w   will one queen
hw   while (some accents)
ʔ   **glottal stop** not a lot (some accents)

The vowel phonemes of English are as follows:

i:	p<u>ea</u>ce
ɪ	k<u>i</u>t
ɛ	b<u>e</u>d
a	b<u>a</u>d
u:	f<u>oo</u>d
ʊ	f<u>oo</u>t
ʌ	b<u>u</u>d
ɒ	l<u>o</u>t
ɔ:	th<u>ou</u>ght
ɑ:	f<u>a</u>ther
ɛ:	t<u>er</u>m
ə	<u>a</u>bout
eɪ	s<u>ay</u>
aɪ	tr<u>y</u>
ɔɪ	j<u>oy</u>
oʊ	s<u>oa</u>p
aʊ	h<u>ou</u>se

When symbols appear between slanted lines, e.g. /a/, this indicates these sounds have the status of **phoneme**. When they appear like this [a], no claim is being made about their status as phonemes. Transcriptions between this type of bracket [ ] are therefore being used to show various aspects of the phonetic detail of the speaker's pronunciation.

Conventions used in the transcripts

1 + indicates a pause by the speaker (any length)
   (Pauses are not given in the transcripts when there are tasks or exercises which ask users to listen for pauses.)
2 (?) is used when the spelling of a word is uncertain
3 (unintell) is used when a speaker's words are unintelligible
4 In a conversation between two or more people, the speech of the person who does not have the speaking turn, but is agreeing or making 'feedback noises' appears in parentheses. For example: 'and I went to live with my grandmother (yeah) who lived in the next village . . .'
5 . . . is used to show that some words have not been included in the transcript
6 Hesitation noises or filled pauses are spelled 'um' or 'uh'
7 Agreement noises are spelled 'uhhuh'

8 When there is overlapping speech between two people conversing, separate lines of text will be used to capture the co-ordination or overlap of the speaking turns, e.g.:

> and my children were + fascinated by their new sister
> excited when they saw her

Symbol chart of the International Phonetic Association

THE INTERNATIONAL PHONETIC ALPHABET (revised to 1993, corrected 1996)

CONSONANTS (PULMONIC)

	Bilabial	Labiodental	Dental	Alveolar	Postalveolar	Retroflex	Palatal	Velar	Uvular	Pharyngeal	Glottal
Plosive	p b			t d		ʈ ɖ	c ɟ	k g	q ɢ		ʔ
Nasal	m	ɱ		n		ɳ	ɲ	ŋ	ɴ		
Trill	ʙ			r					ʀ		
Tap or Flap				ɾ		ɽ					
Fricative	ɸ β	f v	θ ð	s z	ʃ ʒ	ʂ ʐ	ç ʝ	x ɣ	χ ʁ	ħ ʕ	h ɦ
Lateral fricative				ɬ ɮ							
Approximant		ʋ		ɹ		ɻ	j	ɰ			
Lateral approximant				l		ɭ	ʎ	ʟ			

Where symbols appear in pairs, the one to the right represents a voiced consonant. Shaded areas denote articulations judged impossible.

CONSONANTS (NON-PULMONIC)

Clicks		Voiced implosives		Ejectives	
ʘ	Bilabial	ɓ	Bilabial	ʼ	Examples:
ǀ	Dental	ɗ	Dental/alveolar	pʼ	Bilabial
ǃ	(Post)alveolar	ʄ	Palatal	tʼ	Dental/alveolar
ǂ	Palatoalveolar	ɠ	Velar	kʼ	Velar
ǁ	Alveolar lateral	ʛ	Uvular	sʼ	Alveolar fricative

VOWELS

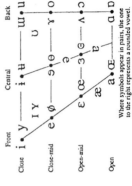

Where symbols appear in pairs, the one to the right represents a rounded vowel.

OTHER SYMBOLS

ʍ Voiceless labial-velar fricative	ɕ ʑ Alveolo-palatal fricatives
w Voiced labial-velar approximant	ɺ Alveolar lateral flap
ɥ Voiced labial-palatal approximant	ʃ and X
ʜ Voiceless epiglottal fricative	
ʢ Voiced epiglottal fricative	Affricates and double articulations can be represented by two symbols joined by a tie bar if necessary. k͡p t͡s
ʡ Epiglottal plosive	

DIACRITICS   Diacritics may be placed above a symbol with a descender, e.g. ŋ̊

Voiceless	n̥ d̥	Breathy voiced	b̤ a̤	Dental	t̪ d̪
Voiced	s̬ t̬	Creaky voiced	b̰ a̰	Apical	t̺ d̺
Aspirated	tʰ dʰ	Linguolabial	t̼ d̼	Laminal	t̻ d̻
More rounded	ɔ̹	Labialized	tʷ dʷ	Nasalized	ẽ
Less rounded	ɔ̜	Palatalized	tʲ dʲ	Nasal release	dⁿ
Advanced	u̟	Velarized	tˠ dˠ	Lateral release	dˡ
Retracted	e̱	Pharyngealized	tˤ dˤ	No audible release	d̚
Centralized	ë	Velarized or pharyngealized	ɫ		
Mid-centralized	ě	Raised	e̝ (ɹ̝ = voiced alveolar fricative)		
Syllabic	n̩	Lowered	e̞ (β̞ = voiced bilabial approximant)		
Non-syllabic	e̯	Advanced Tongue Root	e̘		
Rhoticity	ɚ a˞	Retracted Tongue Root	e̙		

SUPRASEGMENTALS

ˈ	Primary stress
ˌ	Secondary stress
	ˌfoʊnəˈtɪʃən
ː	Long eː
ˑ	Half-long eˑ
˘	Extra-short ĕ
|	Minor (foot) group
‖	Major (intonation) group
.	Syllable break ɹi.ækt
‿	Linking (absence of a break)

TONES AND WORD ACCENTS

LEVEL		CONTOUR	
e̋ or ˥	Extra high	ě or ˩˥	Rising
é ˦	High	ê ˥˩	Falling
ē ˧	Mid	e᷄ ˦˥	High rising
è ˨	Low	e᷅ ˩˨	Low rising
ȅ ˩	Extra low	e᷈ ˧˦˨	Rising-falling
ꜜ	Downstep	↗	Global rise
ꜛ	Upstep	↘	Global fall

Acknowledgements

This book would not have been possible without the contributions of the following people, and I would like to express my thanks to them for their interest, help and generosity.

Paul Tench, of the Centre for Language and Communication, Cardiff University, for acting as consultant for the transcriptions. His advice and suggestions were invaluable.

Barbara Bradford, of the School of Oriental and African Studies, University of London, for her comments on the material in Unit 11, and for providing the recording here entitled 'elephant highways'.

Professor Peter Roach, of the Department of Linguistic Science, University of Reading, for providing the computer-manipulated speech used in Unit 6.

Professor Henry Widdowson, of the University of Vienna, for permission to use extracts from his book, *Practical Stylistics*, and for providing recordings of a selection of the poems for Unit 5.

The Players of St. Peter, Olive Stubbs, David Coster, Eileen Mills, Peter L. Evans, and Ted Weddon, for providing a recording of one of their rehearsal sessions.

Charity Scott-Stokes, of the University of Cambridge, for providing the readings used in Unit 3.

I would like to thank the following people for agreeing to be tape-recorded and/or for providing recordings used in this book: Frances Brodie, Hely Cavalcante, Margaret Dadzie, Mungo Frost, Pat Harvey, James MacKenzie, Amanda Maitland, Aaron Rizhik, Seamus O'Coilcain, Olive Stubbs.

The source of the recordings used in Units 1 and 2 was **The National Sound Archive of the British Library** in London.

The source of the recording here entitled 'siracucus' in Unit 11 was A. Hughes and P. Trudgill, *English Accents and Dialects*, 3rd edn (London, Arnold, 1996).

Finally, I would like to thank Christina Wipf Perry, editor at Arnold, for her advice and support.

'the sound of the human voice'

In this first unit we will be examining the basic types of sounds used in English (and all languages) – **consonants** and **vowels**. To study pronunciation, we need to look at how the sounds of English are produced, and to do this we will need to study the process known as 'articulation'. Like any discipline, phonetics needs descriptive categories, so this unit will review the terminology needed to describe vowels and consonants, and the special set of symbols that have been designed to represent speech sounds, the International Phonetic Alphabet (IPA). Before working on this unit, it is useful to have studied the vocal organs – the organs of speech, and to have a general idea of how sounds are made. But some basic concepts and issues will be explained as they are introduced, and terms defined.

Background

The speaker in this recording is a Jamaican-born writer. She was recorded delivering a lecture at a conference on Caribbean Writing held in London. In her lecture she talks about her upbringing in Jamaica, and the way her childhood has influenced her poetry and prose writing.

What is 'voice'?

At one point in her lecture, the speaker says '. . . the sound of the human voice is important to me . . .'. She is talking in general about spoken language, but in phonetics, the term 'voice' has a special meaning. It is used to refer to the vibration of the vocal cords in the larynx or 'voice box'. The energy for speech comes from the air in the lungs; as our chest muscles force air from the lungs through the larynx, we can make the **vocal cords** vibrate, producing **voice**. A comparison can be made with certain musical instruments, such as the clarinet or oboe. Forcing air through the mouthpiece sets up a vibration which is part of the 'sound' of the instrument. Speech sounds created in this way are 'voiced'; sounds produced without this vibration are 'voiceless'.

We will begin by looking at a category of consonant sounds which are made using voice.

Exercise 1

Nasal consonants

Two of the consonants in English which use voice are the sounds spelled with the letters 'm' and 'n'. As well as involving vocal cord vibration, these sounds also involve the use of a resonating chamber, much like the space inside a clarinet or the wooden body of a guitar. In the case of this type of consonant, the resonating chamber is the nasal cavity, so the term **nasal** consonant is used to describe their **manner of articulation**.

Listen to this excerpt from the early part of her lecture, where the speaker talks about her early childhood. She has explained that she was born in a small village, but at the age of four was adopted by a member of her mother's family, and lived sometimes in the village, and sometimes in the city.

Sequence 1

> I spent my early childhood um shifting back and forth between these two environments + which + uh represent + in a way the polarities in Jamaican life because with my parents I lived in a small village + which was essentially black + peasant + and where + the the African heritage the folk heritage was very strong + um in
> 5 my other life + I lived in a situation where I was an only child + and um a lonely child because really I didn't even have companions to play with + and I was being socialised into + the + um European values of our society

Question 1

Find examples of words with 'm' and 'n'. These two sounds are made by creating an obstruction in the mouth, forcing the air from the lungs to flow into the nasal cavity. The IPA symbols are /m/ and /n/. Say these words yourself and try to feel how the obstruction is created in the mouth.

Question 2

The third sound in English which belongs to this category occurs at the end of the word 'shifting'. Find the other words which end with this sound, and try to feel where the obstruction is made for this nasal consonant. (The symbol is /ŋ/.)

Question 3

The vowel sounds in English are voiced, so if a word has only vowels and nasal consonants, the vocal cords are vibrating throughout the pronunciation of that word. Find the words in the sequence which:

(a) begin with a vowel and end with a nasal;
(b) begin with a nasal and end with a vowel;
(c) end with a vowel (disregard the other sounds).

Exercise 2

Plosive consonants

This type of consonant sound is made by creating an obstruction in the mouth and then suddenly releasing the air from the lungs that has been prevented from escaping by the obstruction. Unlike nasal consonants, which you can extend as long as you have breath, **plosive** sounds are like quick ex**plos**ions. The obstruction can be made with the lips, as in /p/ and /b/. These are called **bi-labial** plosives. It can be made with the tongue, with its tip just behind the teeth at the **alveolar ridge**, for /t/ and /d/, or with the back and sides of the tongue held tightly against the upper teeth and the soft palate or **velum**, for /k/ and /g/. So English has a basic system of six plosives at three different **places of articulation**:

bi-labial	alveolar	velar
/p/ and /b/	/t/ and /d/	/k/ and /g/

Sequence 2

In this part of her lecture, the speaker talks about what she read as a child, and the importance of storytelling in her early life. (There's a break at line 10.)

um I'm not sure I really understood much of what I read but I fell in love with the
word + not just with the printed word + but with the spoken word and I think um
this has greatly influenced the way I write + because again in the village + um I
wasn't reading very much except of course the Bible which we were forced to read
5   + um but I was listening + talk was very important + this was a situation where we
had no no no media + I mean maybe one person in the village had a radio we
certainly didn't I mean that was a big luxury + television of course was unknown
we didn't have cinemas + and we were forced + into into ourselves to provide our
own entertainment + so there were lots of concerts + um you know that kind of thing
10   but + what was most important was the storytelling – a lot of children became
storytellers + because any- anything that happened in the village any little bit of
gossip + any any strange activity + became the the um fodder for your imagination
and for your dramatic skills + and the the children who were + um regarded as
valuable by their parents were the ones who + could 'talk story good' you know +
15   I I wasn't good at that because as a child I was + um I didn't talk much actually
but it's + looking back I clearly listened + I listened a lot and I took in everything

Question 1

Find some examples in the sequence of these sounds at the beginning of words.

Question 2

Several words in the extract have more than one plosive. Find the words which
fit the following patterns. 'V' stands for any vowel sound, and 'N' for any nasal
consonant.

(a) bi-labial V alveolar
(b) bi-labial V velar
(c) velar V N alveolar
(d) alveolar V velar

Question 3

Listen to the sequence and decide how many plosives each of the following
words has. (Line references precede each word.)

(a) 1 understood	**(b)** 2 printed	**(c)** 5 listening				
(d) 5 important	**(e)** 6 village	**(f)** 7 luxury	**(g)** 7 unknown
(h) 9 concerts	**(i)** 12 strange	**(j)** 12 activity				
(k) 12 imagination	**(l)** 13 dramatic	**(m)** 13 children				

Question 4

The six plosives can be divided into voiced and voiceless pairs. /p/, /t/ and /k/ are voiceless, and /b/, /d/ and /g/ are voiced.

Listen to the following words and decide which plosive is used at the end of each. (Line references precede each word.)

(a) 2 printed   (b) 3 influenced   (c) 4 forced
(d) 11 happened   (e) 13 regarded   (f) 16 listened

Question 5

When a word starts with any of the plosives followed immediately by a vowel, the difference between the pairs of plosives is not so much whether there is vocal cord vibration or not, but when it begins in the production of the consonant plus vowel combination. With /b/, /d/ and /g/ the vocal cord vibration begins during and as the obstruction is released and carries on for the vowel sound; with /p/, /t/ and /k/, there is a delay before the vibration begins for the vowel, and this delay is 'filled' with the sound of the expulsion of a puff of air, or **aspiration**.

Listen again to words in the sequence that begin with /p/, /t/, or /k/ immediately before a vowel, and try to hear the short period of aspiration.

Question 6

In words where /p/, /t/, or /k/ occur in combination with another consonant, as in 'spoken', English speakers do **not** use aspiration. Listen to the word 'story-telling' in the sequence. Notice how in 'telling' there will be aspiration associated with the /t/, but in 'story', there is not. If you have difficulty hearing this difference, try to say the word 'story' by making the first sound, and then saying the word 'Tory'. Or try the same with 'skill' and 'kill', or with 'spoke' and 'poke'.

Question 7

When plosive consonants are at the end of a word and the next sound is a vowel sound, English speakers make a smooth link between the consonant and the vowel. Listen to the following groups of words and notice the way the speaker links these sounds. (These are in order of occurrence.)

(a) but I fell
(b) with the spoken word and
(c) had a radio
(d) provide our own
(e) that kind of thing
(f) a lot of
(g) bit of gossip
(h) regarded as valuable
(i) good at that
(j) looking back I clearly
(k) took in everything

Question 8

When producing plosives, sometimes a speaker will not release the closure or contact between the lips, or tongue and the roof of the mouth. In other words, the closure is held, and the speaker articulates the next sound, whatever that is, without having released the plosive. Listen to the way the speaker says the phrase 'talk story good'. You should be able to hear the release stages of the plosives /k/ and /d/. But when she says 'I didn't talk much', she doesn't release the plosive /k/ in 'talk'.

Now listen to these words on the following lines and see if you can hear whether they are released or unreleased. The diacritic used for unreleased plosives is [˺].

(a) 3 the way I write
(b) 4 except of course the Bible
(c) 5 talk was very important
(d) 12 any strange activity

Fricatives

The next category of consonants are made with the tongue, teeth, or roof of the mouth positioned very close to each other so that when the air is expelled from the lungs, it is squeezed through this small space. The result is the sound we associate with air under pressure escaping – a hiss or rush of air. This category of consonant sound is given the label **fricative**. Fricatives can be made with voicing or without.

Exercise 3

Question 1

Listen to the first four lines of Sequence 3 up to the words 'pure narrative'. There are several words with an 's' in the spelling. All of these words use an alveolar fricative. The tongue is positioned very close to the alveolar ridge. Listen to these words and decide whether the fricative you hear is voiced or voiceless.

Sequence 3

In this extract the speaker is talking about how her writing is changing.

the sound of the human voice is important to me + and I think as a writer increasingly I + am + conscious of the power of narrative + and I find increasingly my
work is becoming more and more + both my poetry and my prose + is becoming
more and more pure narrative in other words I'm trying to + ease myself as a writer
5 out of the situation and just let my characters speak for themselves + and it's
wonderful growing up in a society + which + um + has such a + a range of
language + you know because it it does give you um this + this wide range of
expression from which to to choose + and more and more I I find I am attempting
to plunge deeper and deeper into the consciousness of my characters or they're doing
10 it for me because I'm allowing them to + to + you know + express more and more
and more of what's + what's inside them and in this way I'm hoping that the characters can + can transcend the limitations of the printed page and leap + to meet
the consciousness of the reader

Question 2

Are there any other words in these lines which have an alveolar fricative?

Question 3

Now check the rest of the sequence for voiced and voiceless alveolar fricatives.

Another pair of fricatives used in English are /f/ and /v/. These sounds are made by bringing the upper front teeth and lower lip very close together. Because of the involvement of the lips and teeth, they are called **labio-dental** fricatives. They are usually spelled with the letters 'f' and 'v'.

Question 4

The voiced labio-dental fricative occurs at the beginning of the word 'voice' and the voiceless one occurs at the beginning of the word 'find'. Find the other words in the sequence which have these sounds.

Question 5

English also has two fricatives which are made with the tongue and the teeth very close together. These are called **dental** fricatives. Again there are both voiced and voiceless ones. Both are represented in the spelling of English words with the two letters 'th'. Find all the words in this sequence with this spelling. Can you hear which have the voiceless consonant /θ/ and which have the voiced one /ð/?

The final pair of fricatives are made with quite a complicated arrangement of the articulators. There is a groove down the centre of the tongue; the tip of the tongue is near the alveolar ridge, and the middle area of the tongue is near the **hard palate**. In many cases the lips are pursed or rounded. The label given to this pair of sounds is **palato-alveolar**.

Question 6

Listen to the words 'express' and 'expression'. The first has a voiceless alveolar consonant represented by the double 's', but the second does not, despite the spelling. This sound is a voiceless palato-alveolar fricative. Its symbol is /ʃ/. Find the other words in this sequence with this sound.

Question 7

There are no examples of the partner sound, the voiced palato-alveolar fricative in this sequence, but there is one example in Sequence 2. Its symbol is /ʒ/. Can you find it?

Exercise 4

Use the symbols in the exercises so far to transcribe the following words from Sequence 3. For vowel sounds simply use the letter 'V'. (They are listed in order of occurrence.)

(a) think
(b) becoming
(c) ease
(d) society
(e) because
(f) attempting
(g) inside

Exercise 5

In Exercise 1 we looked at the nasal consonants of English /m/, /n/ and /ŋ/, and saw that these are made at three different places of articulation, bi-labial, alveolar, and velar. In the pronunciation of English sounds are often modified depending on the other sounds that co-occur with them. For example, an /n/ can be influenced by the articulation of the next consonant. When the speaker says 'increasingly' in Sequence 3, she uses a velar nasal, not an alveolar one. Her articulation of the first nasal is influenced by the velar plosive /k/. Let's look at some other examples where the word 'in' or the syllable 'in-' occurs.

Listen to the following words or phrases in Sequence 3 and try to decide what kind of nasal is being made.

(a) 9 into
(b) 11 inside
(c) 11 in this way

Exercise 6

The next type of consonant is a kind of hybrid. In the phrase 'which has such a range of language' there are four occurrences of this type. At the end of the words 'which' and 'such' the speaker makes a voiceless sound, represented in the spelling with the letters 'ch'. To make this sound the articulators are positioned to make /t/, but then instead of lowering the tongue quickly and completely to let the air escape, the tongue stays close to the roof of the mouth and therefore friction results, just like in fricative consonants. These are called **affricates.** The symbol for the voiceless one is /tʃ/, and for the voiced one at the end of the words 'range' and 'language' it is /dʒ/. Find the other words in the sequence which have these sounds.

Exercise 7

The liquids

Listen to Sequence 4. There are many examples of sounds which are spelled with 'l' and 'r'. This category of sound is typically made with voicing and with unhindered airflow so the oral cavity still acts as a resonating chamber. But there can still be some type of obstruction in the oral tract. When this speaker makes an /l/ sound, the tip of the tongue will be touching the alveolar ridge, but the sides of the tongue will be drawn in so that the air can pass around the sides. For the 'r' sound there will be a groove down the middle of the tongue while the body of the tongue is drawn back and humped up.

Sequence 4

In this extract the speaker talks about the importance of reading in Caribbean society.

> one of the things I discovered early was that + if you walked around with a book in your hand + people left you alone because they figured + you couldn't get into trouble [laughter] you know so I always had a book in my hand at first + everybody admired me greatly they'd say 'Lord look a girl her reading' [laughter] and
> 5 you know um it it was a weapon + that I used + to distance myself from from an environment that I found painful and hard to deal with + you know and um I think this is still true of the society that that people people respect book-learning and children + are still um encouraged to get an education and um + including girl children you know it's something that's very very powerful in Caribbean society

Exercise 8

The glides

The word 'you' occurs several times in this sequence. This word begins with a sound which has no obstruction in the oral cavity. This sound is voiced and its quality is produced by the resonance created when the body of the tongue is hunched up near the hard palate.

Question 1

Can you find another word with this sound in the sequence which *isn't* spelled with the letter 'y'?

There are two glides in English: the one discussed above is labelled as **palatal** because of the position of the tongue near the hard palate; the second has a very complex articulation. The tongue is pulled back and hunched up as for /k/, and the lips are rounded. The label used is **labio-velar**. In English it is usually represented by the letter 'w'.

Question 2

Listen to the speaker's pronunciation of these words. Does she use voicing when she produces this glide? (Line references precede each word.)

(a) 1 was
(b) 1 walked
(c) 1 with
(d) 3 always
(e) 5 weapon
(f) 9 powerful

Exercise 9

There are three words in the sequence that begin with the letter 'h' – 'hand', 'had' and 'hard'. This consonant sound only occurs in English at the beginning of a word or a syllable preceding a vowel sound, as we see in all of these words. It can be described as a period of voicelessness before a vowel. There is no fricative-like narrowing in the mouth, so the greatest point of narrowing is in the larynx.

Looking back

In this unit we have reviewed the consonant system of English, and examined the basic set of consonant sounds or **phonemes**. We have also reviewed the articulatory processes involved in producing consonants. We have also begun to look at two important pronunciation processes: the way the pronunciation of consonants can be modified according to adjacent sounds, and the way sounds are linked to each other in the stream of speech.

Tasks for consolidation or discussion

Choose any type or pair of consonant sounds, e.g. nasals, or voiced and voiceless fricatives, and choose one of the sequences to carry out a search for these sounds.

Select some words at random from a sequence, or choose, say, every fifth word. Refer to the transcripts to make a description of the consonants in your words, giving the labels for each one. Then listen carefully to the speaker pronouncing these words and check your description. (Remember that the spelling of a word can be deceptive!)

Unit I Key and comments

EXERCISE I   Question 1

Some words are: betwee**n** Ja**m**aica**n** **m**y s**m**all. For /m/ the obstruction is made by closing the lips; for /n/ it is made by placing the tongue against the roof of the mouth. The tip is held against the ridge just behind the front teeth (the **alveolar ridge**) and the sides of the tongue are held near the upper molars.

These two positions give us the terms **labial** (involving the lips) and **alveolar** (involving the alveolar ridge).

EXERCISE I   Question 2

There are two other words: stro**ng** and bei**ng** The back of the tongue is held tightly against the soft muscular area of the roof of the mouth, called the **velum**. Sounds that are made involving the velum are called **velar**.

EXERCISE I   Question 3

(a) in an and Notice that each of the three times the speaker says the word 'and' the word ends with the nasal sound. She does not pronounce the 'd'.

(b) my

(c) two way the only lonely to society

EXERCISE 2 <u>Question 1</u>

/p/ printed person provide parents
/b/ Bible big but because bit back
/t/ talk to television took
/d/ didn't dramatic
/k/ course concert kind could clearly
/g/ greatly gossip

EXERCISE 2 <u>Question 2</u>

(a) but bit
(b) big back
(c) kind good
(d) talk took

EXERCISE 2 <u>Question 3</u>

(a) under<u>stoo</u>d   **(b)** <u>print</u>ed   **(c)** none   **(d)** im<u>portan</u>t   **(e)** none
(f) Can you hear the /g/ in this word?   **(g)** none   **(h)** <u>concerts</u>
(i) none   **(j)** a<u>ctivity</u>   **(k)** none   **(l)** <u>dramatic</u>   **(m)** none

(Note that she does not use a /d/ in her pronunciation.)

EXERCISE 2 <u>Question 4</u>

(a) /d/   **(b)** /t/   **(c)** /t/   **(d)** /d/   **(e)** /d/   **(f)** /d/

EXERCISE 2 <u>Question 5</u>

One way to demonstrate the aspiration is to hold a feather or slip of paper in front of your lips and say a word beginning with /p/ and then a word beginning with /b/. The puff of air for /p/ should make the feather or paper move. With /b/ it will not move. This aspiration is also apparent not just at the beginning of words but in any part of a word where /p/, /t/, or /k/ precedes a vowel, as in 'apart', 'attack', or 'account'.

EXERCISE 2 <u>Question 6</u>

Use the aspiration test again to check that there is no puff of air in words like 'spoke', 'speak', 'spend', etc. It doesn't work so well with words with /t/ or /k/

because the air pressure is reduced by the time it reaches the feather as the obstruction for these sounds is further back in the mouth.

EXERCISE 2 Question 7

This linkage is represented sometimes in spellings such as 'kinda' or 'lotta'.

EXERCISE 2 Question 8

(a) released
(b) notice that the /p/ before the /t/ is not released
(c) the final /t/ is released
(d) the /k/ after the vowel (represented by 'c' in the spelling) is not released

EXERCISE 3 Question 1

voiceless: sound increasingly conscious
voiced: prose

EXERCISE 3 Question 2

The word 'voice' has a voiceless alveolar fricative at the end, and the words 'as' and 'is' have voiced alveolar fricatives.

EXERCISE 3 Question 3

/s/	/z/
myself	words
situation	ease
just	as
speak	characters
themselves	themselves
it's	has
society	because
such	does
this	choose
consciousness	limitations
what's	
inside	
transcend	
express	

Note that the letter 'x' in 'express' stands for a sequence of /k/ followed by /s/.

EXERCISE 3   **Question 4**

/f/	/v/
mysel<u>f</u>	o<u>f</u>
wonder<u>f</u>ul	gi<u>v</u>e
<u>f</u>rom	themsel<u>v</u>es

EXERCISE 3   **Question 5**

/θ/	/ð/
think	the
both	other
	this
	they're
	them
	that
	themselves

EXERCISE 3   **Question 6**

situation limitation The spelling 'ti' stands for a /ʃ/ sound.

EXERCISE 3   **Question 7**

The word is 'televi<u>s</u>ion'.

EXERCISE 4

(a) θvŋk	**(b)** bvkvmvŋ	**(c)** vz	**(d)** svsvvtv
(e) bvkvz	**(f)** vtvmp˺tvŋ	**(g)** vnsvd	

EXERCISE 5   **Question 1**

(a) alveolar   **(b)** alveolar   **(c)** dental

There are more examples in Sequence 2. When the speaker says 'in the' at line 11, she also uses a dental nasal, and in the word 'influenced' at line 3 the nasal will be labio-dental due to the labio-dental consonant.

EXERCISE 6

plunge choose page just

EXERCISE 8 <u>Question 1</u>

used

EXERCISE 8 <u>Question 2</u>

In all these words the /w/ is voiced.

EXERCISE 9

/h/ has also been described as a 'glottal fricative' in some discussions. See, for example, Davenport and Hannahs (1998) section 3.3 or Roach (1991) section 4.1. It has also been termed a 'glottal glide' (see Kreidler (1997: 53)).

See PE5 Sections 9.1 to 9.8 for a full discussion of the English consonants.

'he was a gent was my father'

Preview

In this unit the main focus will be on the vowels of English. As in Unit 1, we will review the basic articulatory processes and use the recordings to investigate the pronunciation of vowel sounds. Having covered both vowel and consonant sounds, we can then examine the structure of syllables. One of the consonant sounds discussed in Unit 1 will be examined in more detail.

Background

The speaker in this recording was born in 1923 and is a doctor. He has worked all his life as a general practitioner, a 'family doctor', in the north of England, mainly in the city of Sheffield. He was being interviewed as a part of a collection of material on the history of General Practice. In this part of the interview he is questioned about his parents and his early life and experiences.

How do we make vowels?

The production of vowels does not depend on any obstruction in the vocal tract, or any narrowing sufficient to cause friction. The quality of a particular vowel is determined by the shape of the vocal tract, that is, its resonating chamber. This shape is produced by the position of the lips, which can be rounded, or pursed, or spread or neutrally open. It is also determined by the position of the tongue, whether it is raised or lowered, and what part of the roof of the mouth it is near.

The position of the jaw will also determine the shape of the resonating chamber. If the jaw is lowered, then there is a larger space in the oral cavity. This information can be most easily captured and represented on a vowel chart, as seen on the IPA symbols page.

Exercise 1

We'll begin with a vowel that is very easy to describe, because it is produced with the tongue in a 'rest' or neutral position, and the lips slightly open. It is also the most frequent vowel that is used in English.

Listen to the two phrases the doctor uses to describe his father. There are seven occurrences of this 'neutral' vowel, which is given the name 'schwa'. The symbol is /ə/. The letter underlined shows where the speaker uses this vowel.

a̠ man tha̠t I greatly re̠spect̠e̠d uh a̠ man o̠f great integrity

Sequence 1

The interviewer has asked him: 'What sort of man was your father?'

a man that I greatly respected + uh a man of great integrity + who knew his job inside and out + um who could + go and buy + he was a butcher + uh he could go and buy the cattle + buy the sheep and pigs + uh do the slaughtering + preparation work he c- was the complete butcher + not the purveyor of meat that you have now
5 + uh he could do the whole lot + and uh + he was a gent + was my father + yes + I had great admiration and respect for him + and uh + the other thing was that they + always said 'you do what you want' + you know you fulfil yourself + intellectually as much as you can and we'll support you as much as we can afford + and whatever you want to be we'll try and do it for you

Which of the following words in the sequence also have a schwa?

complete   purveyor   afford   support

Exercise 2

Front vowels

If the tongue is pulled forward from neutral position and close to the roof of the mouth, the vowels that are produced are termed 'high front' or 'close' vowels.

There are two vowels in English produced in this way, and they are illustrated in the phrase 'sheep and pigs'.

Listen to this phrase and notice the difference between the vowel in 'sheep', for which we'll use the symbol /i:/, and the vowel in 'pigs', symbolized by /ɪ/. If you try to make these yourself you'll feel that the lips are slightly spread.

Question 1

Find two words in the sequence with /i:/ followed by a voiceless alveolar plosive.

Question 2

Find three words in the sequence where /ɪ/ is followed by a nasal consonant.

The doctor describes his father as a 'gent'. The vowel in this word is also a front vowel, but the tongue is lower than for /i:/ or /ɪ/. Its symbol is /ɛ/. The speaker uses this vowel in the following words:

said   intellectually   respect   integrity   whatever

If the tongue is lowered even further (and the jaw dropped very slightly along with this movement) the vowel /a/ is produced. This can be termed a low front vowel. The words 'man' and 'cattle' have this vowel, as does the word 'admiration'. It is usually spelled with the letter 'a' in English.

Question 3

The words 'had', 'have' and 'and' all have an 'a' in the spelling. Does the speaker use the /a/ vowel in these words?

Back vowels

If the tongue is pulled back in the mouth, then the quality of the resonating chamber changes. For this type of vowel, there is usually some degree of lip rounding.

Exercise 3

In Sequence 2 the speaker tells of how he liked to pinch apples from their neighbour's orchard. Listen to his pronunciation of the word 'fruit'.

Sequence 2

The interviewer has asked: 'What would happen if you did something that your parents disapproved of?'

> um well if it was something horrendous I would get a clout + uh but on the whole
> they would sit me down and talk to me + uh and say look you just don't do this
> sort of thing + you know + um I mean we had an orchard + uh next door to the
> house + and uh + I used to climb the fence and pinch the odd apple + uh but the
> 5   uh + our neighbour Mrs O'Neil said 'look Jack + don't climb the fence you'll
> break it + if you just want any fruit just come in and knock on the door and say
> 'I'm going to get an apple' that took all the spice out of it of course [he begins to
> laugh] I never wanted to do it then she was a very astute old lady [laughing] took
> the took the spice away from it there was no fun in it it was just as easy to go to
> 10   the uh apple bowl and + take one

The word 'fruit' has a high back vowel with lip rounding.

🔍 Question 1

Find two other words in the sequence with this vowel followed by a voiceless alveolar plosive. We'll use the symbol /uː/.

The lips are also rounded for the next vowel, but the tongue is not so close to the back of the roof of the mouth. This vowel is /ʊ/ and occurs in the words 'look' and 'took'.

🔍 Question 2

There are several words with the two vowel letters 'ou' in the spelling in the sequence. Do any of them have the /ʊ/ vowel?

would   clout   house   neighbour   course

Another back vowel is /ɔː/ used in the word 'orchard'. This vowel has medium lip rounding, and the tongue is at approximately the same height in the mouth as for /ɛ/.

🔍 Question 3

The quotations in the apple pinching story, by Mrs O'Neil and his parents, contain two words with this vowel. Can you find them?

A further lowering of the tongue and a slight open lip rounding produces a back vowel as in the words 'kn<u>o</u>ck' and 'h<u>o</u>rrendous'. We'll use the symbol /ɒ/.

There is an example in the sequence of the back vowel /ʌ/. It occurs in the word 'fun'. It can also be used in the word 'just', but on the second occasion the speaker uses it in the sequence, it has a schwa.

So far we have looked at examples of 11 different vowels; all of them are termed **monophthongs**, from the Greek words for 'one sound' because there is no variation in the shape assumed by the lips or tongue as these sounds are made. But the English vowel system has several vowels where there is a change of some sort – the lips change position slightly, or the tongue moves slightly, and this produces a varying quality. These vowels are called **diphthongs**. We will use Sequence 3 to study these.

Exercise 4

Listen to the sequence and see if you can hear any vowels with changing quality.

Sequence 3

In this sequence the interviewer is talking to the doctor about his and his parents' involvement in politics. He has asked: 'Did your mother follow the same pattern as your father, politics-wise?'

> mother really wasn't very bothered about politics at all + uh + they were very
> strong + uh family people + and the family + and the widest sense of the relatives
> + was really the thing that uh + made them tick + uh + during the war + um + they
> were + very staunch supporters of uh + Churchill and the government and the war
> 5 effort in general + uh + and uh + but in general terms + they were not + uh active
> political people + my father was lucky you see he was never ever out of work +
> ever in the whole of his life + um he was doing the job he enjoyed doing more than
> anything in the world + he was interested in animals he he loved to ride + um he
> was totally fulfilled and mum was fulfilled looking after dad and me and she had
> 10 no + social ambitions + um she'd got a large family in Bury St Edmonds when we
> lived when I was young + and uh so they were both fulfilled

✑ Question 1

Listen to the example words from the sequence with each of the following diphthongs and then try to find the other words in the sequence where the speaker uses the same diphthong.

The symbols used for diphthongs give an approximate starting and finishing point for each of these vowels.

/eɪ/ 'made'
/oʊ/ 'no'
/aɪ/ 'ride'
/aʊ/ 'out'

Question 2

There is only one word in this sequence with another of the English diphthongs. This word is 'enj<u>oy</u>ed'. The symbol is /ɔɪ/.

Question 3

You may have noticed that this speaker does not pronounce an /r/ consonant sound in words such as 'war' and 'Churchill'. This means that he has another monophthong in his vowel system, like many other speakers with a similar accent to his.

This vowel occurs in the words 'work' and 'terms' in the sequence. The symbol we'll use is /ɛ:/. The symbol /ə:/ is also commonly used.

In the word 'large' he also does not produce an /r/ sound, but the vowel is different. It is the same vowel as in the word 'father'. The symbol is /ɑ:/.

Exercise 5

Practice using the vowel and consonant symbols by transcribing the following words selected from the sequences. Instead of listening to the speaker, say these words to yourself as if you were reading them out from a list.

Sequence 1

(a) buy   **(b)** who   **(c)** slaughtering   **(d)** admiration

Sequence 2

(d) clout   **(e)** next   **(f)** climb   **(g)** spice   **(h)** one

Sequence 3

(i) strong   **(j)** family   **(k)** relatives   **(l)** staunch

Exercise 6

Now that we have discussed all of the basic consonant and vowels of English, we can analyse the typical patterns in which they occur. We'll use some of the words in Exercise 5 to do this.

The shortest words that are possible in English are ones that have only a vowel sound, so the word 'I' is a one-syllable word and is composed of one-vowel sound. There are also words which are composed of a single consonant sound before the vowel, such as 'see' and words that are composed of a single consonant sound after a vowel, such as 'in'. There are also words with one syllable which have *both* a single consonant before the vowel and single consonant after the vowel, such as 'had'. If we use the letters 'V' and 'C' to stand for vowel and consonant, then we could represent these possibilities for the structure of one-syllable words as follows:

V VC   CV   CVC

Question 1

Check for the words in Exercise 5 that have any of these syllable structures.

Each syllable must have a vowel at its core, so we could refer to the vowel as the **nucleus** of the syllable. If there is a consonant before this vowel, it is described as the **onset**; if there is a consonant after the vowel, it can be described as the **coda**.

But it is clear that there are many other possibilities for the structure of one-syllable words in English.

Question 2

Find the one-syllable words in Exercise 5 which have two consonants in the onset or two consonants in the coda, and represent their structure with 'C' and 'V'.

Question 3

There are also one-syllable words which have more than two consonants in the onset or coda. Can you find some examples in Exercise 5?

When we say that two words rhyme, we are referring to the fact that they have exactly the same sound in the nucleus and in the coda positions, for example, 'fun' and 'son' or 'made' and 'played'. For this reason, the nucleus and coda are together are referred to as the **rhyme**.

It is important to study the syllable structure patterns in English and to be able to describe them. When we do, we find that there are constraints and restrictions. For example, the consonant /ŋ/ can never occur at the beginning of a syllable in English – it can never be an onset. Also, onsets are restricted to three consonants and no more.

The analysis of syllable structure in this way also reveals important points about particular vowels and consonants. For example, the glides /w/ and /j/ have been described as being made without any obstruction in the vocal tract (see Unit 1, Exercise 8). But doesn't this make them just like vowels? The answer is no. They *function* like consonant sounds in English – neither can be the nucleus of a syllable, they can only be in the onset position, as in the words 'young', 'yell' and 'wit' and 'well'.

Exercise 7

Two types of /l/

In Sequence 3, the speaker uses several words with the consonant /l/. Listen to the following words in the two sets below and see if you can hear a difference in the pronunciation.

SET 1
(a) all   **(b)** general   **(c)** political   **(d)** whole   **(e)** social

SET 2
(f) lucky   **(g)** loved   **(h)** life   **(i)** looking   **(j)** large

Looking back

In this unit we have reviewed the production of vowels, and identified examples of the pronunciation of these English phonemes in the recording. We have seen that there are two basic types of vowels in English – monophthongs and diphthongs. One of the difficulties in describing 'the vowels of English' is that speakers of English don't all share the same ones. Although we have looked at 16 vowel sounds in this unit, we have not yet covered all of the vowel sounds used by English speakers.

We have seen that vowels and consonants can be defined not only by how they are made but by their function in the syllable. The syllable is an important unit, and we have sketched out a way of analysing the structure of syllables. The discussion of the two types of /l/ has demonstrated how sounds in English can be made in slightly different ways depending on their position in a syllable or word.

Tasks for consolidation or discussion

Think about the consonant and vowel systems in other languages that you know. Does English have a larger or smaller set than those languages? Are you familiar with vowel or consonant sounds in other languages which are not part of the English inventory?

Select more one-syllable words from the sequences (or from any other source) and analyse their syllable structure.

Unit 2 Key and comments

EXERCISE 1

All of these words have the schwa vowel. Notice how this vowel can be spelled with several different vowel letters.

c<u>o</u>mplete   p<u>u</u>rvey<u>o</u>r   <u>a</u>fford   s<u>u</u>pport

EXERCISE 2   Question 1

complete   meat

EXERCISE 2   Question 2

<u>i</u>nside   <u>i</u>ntegrity   th<u>i</u>ng

EXERCISE 2   Question 3

He uses /a/ in 'had' and 'have'. The word 'and' occurs eight times. He uses /a/ when he says 'and uh he was a gent' and at the end of the sequence, 'and whatever you want'. The other six times he pronounces this word with a schwa.

EXERCISE 3   **Question 1**

ast<u>u</u>te   <u>u</u>sed

EXERCISE 3   **Question 2**

Only the word 'would' has this vowel.

EXERCISE 3   **Question 3**

door   sort

EXERCISE 4   **Question 1**

The words are listed in order of occurrence.

/eɪ/   they (several occurrences)
/oʊ/   whole t<u>o</u>tally n<u>o</u> s<u>o</u>cial so both
/aɪ/   w<u>i</u>dest life I
/aʊ/   ab<u>ou</u>t

EXERCISE 5

(a) buy baɪ   **(b)** who hu: **(c)** slaughtering slɔːtərɪŋ
(d) admiration admɪreɪʃən   **(e)** clout klaʊt   **(f)** climb klaɪm
(g) spice spaɪs   **(h)** one wɒn   **(i)** strong strɔːŋ   **(j)** family famɪliː
(k) relatives rɛlətɪvz   **(l)** staunch stɔːntʃ

EXERCISE 6   **Question 1**

'buy' is CV; 'who' is CV; 'one' is CVC

EXERCISE 6   **Question 2**

'clout' is CCVC; 'climb' CCVC (Note that this word ends with one consonant even though there are two consonant letters in the spelling.)

'spice' is CCVC; 'staunch' is CCVCC

EXERCISE 6   **Question 3**

'strong' is CCCVC; 'next' is CVCCC

For a full discussion of this aspect of the English sound system, see PE5 10.9.1. This text does not use the terms 'nucleus', 'coda', 'onset' and 'rhyme'. For texts that do, see for example Kreidler (1997: chapter 6), or Davenport and Hannahs (1998).

There is a difference for this speaker between the /l/ when it occurs at the beginning of words, as in Set 2, and at the end of words as in Set 1. In Set 2 words there will be alveolar contact and nothing more. In Set 1 words, in addition to the alveolar contact, the back of the tongue will be raised towards the velum in approximately the same position as for the back vowel /ʊ/ as in 'took'. This 'velarized' version is sometimes called **dark 'l'** and the non-velarized version is known as **clear 'l'**. For speakers who use these two types of /l/, the clear version also occurs in the middle of words before a vowel. So in the word 'family' the speaker uses a clear /l/. If you listen again to the phrase 'political people' you'll hear him use both the dark version at the end of each word, and the clear version in 'political'.

The speaker in Unit 1 does not use dark 'l'. If you listen to how she pronounces 'people' in Sequence 4 as in 'people respect book-learning', you'll hear that the /l/ at the end of 'people' is not very different to the /l/ in 'learning' – both are clear.

A special symbol can be used for the dark version [ɫ]. But we only need to use this if we want to show phonetic detail. Both the Caribbean writer and the doctor are saying *the same word* when they pronounce 'people' in terms of the phonemes of English, so we can show this by using the transcription /piːpl/ for both.

See PE5 Section 8.9 for a full discussion of English vowels.

The pronunciation of English one thousand years ago

Preview

How did English sound one thousand years ago? By using the evidence of the surviving manuscripts, by tracing the development of the language through later periods and using the knowledge of the ways that sounds tend to change (and the ways that they don't tend to change), linguists who are interested in the history of the language can reconstruct the pronunciation of earlier forms of English. Of course we will never know for certain exactly how accurate these reconstructions are. We will use recordings of the reconstructed pronunciation of English for practice in identifying vowel and consonant sounds. We'll see that the pronunciation of some words has changed a great deal, but that of some others has changed very little.

Background

The following questions and exercises are based on four short texts in 'Old English'. This is the name given to the English used in Britain from approximately the fifth century to the end of the eleventh. The reader of the texts is a fellow in medieval studies at the University of Cambridge.

Sequence 1

The first text is a passage from the Bible, St John's Chapter 14, verses 22, 23. It is printed here as it appears in the surviving manuscripts of the Bible. Below it there is a gloss to help you match some Old English words to Present Day English words. Below that there is a translation into modern English.

Iudas cwæð to him, næs na sē Scariot, Dryhten, hwæt is geworden þat þu wilt þē seolfne geswutelian ūs, næs middanearde?

Se Hælend ondswarade ond cwæð him: 'Gif hwā me lufiað, he hilt min spræce ond min Fæder lufað hine, ond we cumað to him ond we wyrciað eardingstowe mid him.

Iudas cwæð to him, næs na sē Scariot
Judas said to him   not   the Iscariot

Dryhten, hwæt is geworden,
Lord,   how is it come about,

þat þu wilt þē seolfne geswutelian ūs, næs middanearde?
that you will yourself reveal   to us, not to the world

Se Hælend ondswarade ond cwæð him: Gif hwā me lufiað
The Saviour answered   and said to him: if anyone me loves

he hilt   min spræce ond min Fæder lufað hine,
he will keep my words and my Father will love him,

ond we cumað to him   ond we wyrciað   eardingstowe mid him.
and we will come to him   and we make   dwelling-place with him.

Judas saith unto him, not Iscariot, Lord, how is it that thou wilt manifest thyself unto us, and not unto the world? Jesus answered and said unto him: 'If a man love me, he will keep my words, and my Father will love him, and we will come to him, and make our abode with him.'

Exercise 1

Many of the letter symbols used to write Old English are the same as are used today. However, the sounds that they represented were different. Also, as in Present Day English, one letter symbol could be used to represent more than one sound.

Question 1

What sounds does letter 'f' represent:

(a) at the beginning of words (as in 'Fæder')
(b) at the end of words (as in 'gif')
(c) between vowels (as in 'lufað')

Question 2

What sound does letter 'w' (by itself) represent? See for example:

cwæð   geworden   we   wyciað   eardingstowe

What sound does it represent in the combination hw- as in 'hwæt'?

Question 3

Is the vowel sound which is spelled with 'æ' a front vowel or a back vowel? How would you transcribe it?

Question 4

There are two letter symbols that are no longer used in modern English: þ and ð. What type of consonant do they represent (plosive, fricative, nasal, or glide)? What is their *place* of articulation?

Question 5

Here are some pronouns and prepositions from Old English and their modern equivalents. In each case, say how the vowel has changed. (In a few cases there has been no change.)

(a) mid   with
(b) min   mine
(c) is   is
(d) him   him
(e) hwā   who
(f) ūs   us
(g) to   to

Question 6

Compare 'ondswarade' with modern 'answered' – which consonant sounds have been 'lost'?

Sequence 2
A charm for swarming bees

One of the cultural practices during the Old English period in Britain was the use of charms or magic incantations. They were recited in order to protect the speaker from harm, to prevent natural disasters, or as a cure for illness or a remedy against hostile witchcraft. There were charms for a sudden pain, against the theft of cattle, for protection on a journey, and so on. The following charm was used to stop a swarm of bees. People believed that witches could cast a spell on honeybees, who became possessed by them and themselves became witches. The charm was to be recited as the bees were swarming away.

> Sitte ge, sige-wif, sigað to eor þan: næfre ge wilde to wuda fleogan.

> Translation: Sit ye, victorious magic women, sink down to earth: never flee wildly to the forest.

Exercise 2

Make a phonetic transcription of the following words from the charm, and then answer the following questions:

(a) sitte ('sit')
(b) sige-wif ('victorious-women')
(c) sigað ('sink')
(d) wilde ('wildly')
(e) wuda ('woods/forest')

Question 1

How has the pronunciation of the word 'wife' (sige-<u>wif</u>) changed? (This word simply meant 'woman' in Old English, not 'married woman' as it does today.)

Question 2

What consonant sounds does the letter 'g' represent?

Question 3

How would you describe the sound represented by 'eo' (in the words 'eor þan' and 'fleogan')?

Sequence 3

This is a charm for a sudden pain or stitch. During the Old English period, people believed that witches could shoot darts into a person and these would cause a sudden pain. To ease such pains, this charm would be used. The sufferer would first prepare a salve of herbs cooked in butter. This preparation would be applied to the painful part of the body while the charm was recited.

> Scyld ðu ðe nu, þu ðysne nið genesan mote. Ut, lytel spere, gif ðu her inne sie.

> Translation: Shield (protect) yourself now, and you may be saved from the effect of this (i.e. the salve). Out, little spear, if you are in me.

Exercise 3

Transcribe the following words from this charm:

(a) genesan ('survive')
(b) mote ('might')
(c) spere ('spear')

Question 1

What type of vowel is represented by the letter 'y' as in 'scyld'? Can you describe the lip and tongue position?

Question 2

Do the words 'lytel' ('little') and 'ðysne' ('this') have the same vowel?

Sequence 4
A poem on the end of summer

The theme of growing old, with references to the changing seasons and the decline of strength and courage is found in many poems in English. Here is a short stanza from an Old English poem.

> Sumer-hat colað, fold-wela fealleð, feondscipe wealleð, eorð-mægen ealda þ, ellen colað.

(The) summer's heat cools, the riches of the earth begin to fall away, (and) the enemy rages. The might of the earth grows aged, and valour cools.

Exercise 4

How have the vowel sounds in the following words changed:

(a) 'heat' ('h<u>ea</u>t')
(b) 'cool' ('c<u>o</u>lað')
(c) 'fall' (f<u>ea</u>lleð')

Exercise 5

Using the four texts, answer these questions:

Question 1

Are the sounds represented by þ or ð voiced or voiceless

(a) at the end of a word?
(b) between vowels?
(c) at the beginning of a word?

Question 2

What sounds does the letter 's' represent at the beginning or end of a word?

Question 3

How is the letter 's' pronounced when it occurs between two vowels, as in 'gene<u>s</u>an' (Text 3)?

Question 4

What sound does it represent when combined with 'c' as in 'scyld' (Text 3)?

Question 5

What sounds can letter 'c' represent?

⬚ Question 6

Note that the reader pronounces all the /r/ sounds that occur in the spellings used in the manuscripts. How would you describe the articulatory features of the /r/ used by the reader?

Tasks for consolidation or discussion

Make a complete transcription of any of the texts, and, using the recordings as a model, practice reading the text aloud.

Looking back

We have seen that English as it was spoken a thousand years ago sounded very different from Present Day English. Some words only have a different vowel sound, although their consonants have remained the same. Some words are recognizable, whereas others are totally unlike any words in the modern language. Trying to analyse the sounds of an unfamiliar language, in this case a vaguely familiar language, can be useful practice in listening carefully and in using phonetic symbols.

Unit 3 Key and comments

EXERCISE I Question 1

(a) /f/   **(b)** /f/   **(c)** /v/

EXERCISE I Question 2

/w/ the labio-velar glide, but in 'hwæt' and 'hwā' it represents the voiceless version of this sound, with slight friction.

EXERCISE I Question 3

A front vowel /a/ could be used.

EXERCISE I Question 4

These are both dental fricatives /θ/ and /ð/. Note that the IPA has adopted one of these ancient letter symbols to use as a phonetic symbol.

EXERCISE I   **Question 5**

(a) no change /ɪ/
(b) /iː/ to a diphthong /aɪ/
(c) no change
(d) no change
(e) both of these have back vowels, but the Old English word had a low or 'open' back vowel /ɑː/ and Present Day English has a high or 'close' back vowel /uː/
(f) 'us' in Old English had /ʊ/; now the vowel is /ʌ/
(g) the vowels are both back but the modern one is higher /o/ versus /uː/

EXERCISE I   **Question 6**

The underlined consonants have been lost – ondswarade. Depending on the accent of the modern speaker, /r/ may not be pronounced. Note that modern English still retains the letter 'w' in the spelling.

EXERCISE 2

(a) sɪtə   **(b)** siːjəwiːf   **(c)** siːɡɑθ
(d) wɪldə   **(e)** wʊda

EXERCISE 2   **Question 1**

The change is from monophthong to diphthong /iː/ to /aɪ/.

EXERCISE 2   **Question 2**

It can represent /j/ or /g/.

EXERCISE 2   **Question 3**

This might be described as a diphthong, but it could also be described as a sequence of two vowels. In Present Day English a sequence of two vowels can occur in a word such as 'going'.

EXERCISE 3

(a) jənɛzan   **(b)** muːtə   **(c)** spɛra

EXERCISE 3 **Question 1**

This vowel is high and front and made with tight lip rounding. The IPA symbol is /y/.

EXERCISE 3 **Question 2**

In these two words the vowel /ɪ/ is used, not /y/.

EXERCISE 4

(a) Old English /ɑ/ to /iː/
(b) Old English /oʊ/ to /uː/
(c) Old English /ɛ/ followed by /a/ to /ɔː/

EXERCISE 5 **Question 1**

(a) voiceless at the end of words
(b) voiced between vowels
(c) at the beginning of a word either voiced or voiceless

This pattern still seems to exist in Present Day English, with a few differences. For example, only voiced dental fricatives usually occur between vowels, as in 'mother' and 'either', but both voiced and voiceless dental fricatives can now occur at the end of words, as in 'both' and 'breathe'.

EXERCISE 5 **Question 2, 3 and 4**

It represents /s/ at the beginning or end of a word; when between vowels it is voiced /z/; and when combined with 'c' as in 'scyld' it represents /ʃ/ or /k/ in 'Scariot'.

EXERCISE 5 **Question 5**

At the beginning of words it represents /k/. See 'colað' in Text 4 and 'cumað' in Text 1. In 'spræce' (Text 1) it represents the voiceless palato-alveolar affricate /tʃ/.

EXERCISE 5 **Question 6**

The /r/ is pronounced as an alveolar **trill**. The tip of the tongue strikes the alveolar ridge a few times in quick succession. In Present Day English this type of /r/ is used, for example, in some accents of Scottish English.

Text 1 is taken from PE5 p. 73. There is a phonetic transcription given which is reprinted here:

 juːdɑs kwæθ toː hɪm næs nɑː seː skɑriɔt drɪçtən hwæt ɪs jəwɔrdən θæt
θuː wɪlt θeː sylfnə jəswʊtɛlɪjən ʊs næs mɪddɑnɛɑdə seː hæːlənd
ɒndswɑrɔdə ɒnd kwæθ hɪm jɪf hwɑː meː lʊvɑθ heː hɪlt miːnə sprætʃə ɒnd
miːn fædər lʊvɑθ hɪnə ɒnd weː kʊmɑθ toː hɪm ɒnd weː wyrkɪɑθ
ɛərdʊŋstoːwə mɪd hɪm

Texts 2, 3 and 4 are from C. L. Wrenn (1967: 150, 168–9).

'you're being silly'

Preview

In this unit we look at the way speakers use the **pitch** of their voices to convey meaning. This aspect of the pronunciation of English is called **intonation**. It is very complex, and this particular recording has been chosen to work on it because the speakers' utterances are relatively short and simple, with several repetitions of the same type of exchange – a statement by one speaker followed by a response from the other.

Background

This is a recording of a grandmother playing with her grandson, who is two years and eight months old. They are in her home, and are looking at one of his picture books. The book is typical of many for children of this age – it has brightly coloured pictures of common objects and animals, sometimes in multiples. Grandmother and grandson often look through this book together, name the objects, talk about colour and shape and how many there are. However, on this occasion the grandmother has purposely decided to **mis**name the objects, to see how her grandson reacts.

Sequence I

('G' stands for the grandmother and 'C' for the child.)

    C: a car
    G: it's a big red ball
    C: no a car

G: oh ok   I think that's two dogs
5   C: no ducks
G: two dogs
C: no ducks
G: ducks   oh ok   how about those I think they are bananas
C: no are apples
10   G: apples   they're apples
C: um   um um tomatoes
G: oh   they're tomatoes   well they do look like tomatoes don't they
C: yeah
G: they are cars
15   C: no are boats
G: they're cars
C: no they boats
G: oh I'm sorry   I'm not very good at this   ok they are
I think they are trucks
20   C: no are balls
G: there's five trucks there
C: no are balls
G: they're balls
C: yeah
25   G: oh let me see if I can do better on this one
these are little boys
C: no are ice creams
G: they're little boys
C: no are ice creams
30   G: they're ice creams
C: yeah
G: oh ok
C: you're silly
G: I'm what   I'm silly
35   C: yeah
G: oh   that's not very nice is it   ok these are books
C: no they're lollipops
G: one two three four five six seven books
C: no no are apples
40   G: they're apples now are they   they're apples   I think they're books
C: no they're not   they're not   'cause are lollipops

G: oh ok I'll take your word for it now these are one two
three four five six seven eight little girls
C: no are butterflies
45 **G:** they're butterflies
C: yeah
G: you sure
C: yeah
G: oh ok
50 **C:** you're being silly
G: I'm being very silly   now these are one two three
four five six seven eight nine apples
C: no are strawberries
G: they're strawberries
55 **C:** yeah
G: how do you know they're strawberries
C: you're being silly
G: I'm a very silly grandma I know
C: you you don't know
60 **G:** I don't know what
C: you don't know the words

. . .

What is intonation?

As we have seen, the sound that we call 'voice' is produced by the vibration of
the vocal cords in the larynx. The vocal cords can vibrate at different speeds; we
perceive this vibration as 'pitch'. The faster the vibration, the higher is the pitch
we hear, and the slower the vibration, the lower is the pitch we hear. Because the
speed of the vibration can change over a syllable, we can have a rising pitch or
tone as the speed increases, and a falling pitch or tone, as the speed decreases.
Pitch height – high, mid, low – and pitch fluctuation – rising, falling, rising then
falling, etc. – are the basic elements of intonation.

Intonation as a system of meaning

As we speak the pitch of our voices is constantly changing on the voiced sounds
– vowels, voiced fricatives, nasals, and so on. We seem to hear this extending

through the voiceless sounds as well, and the perception is of gliding up and down, like a melody. As we move to the end of an utterance, it is natural for the vibration of the vocal cords to decrease, and the voice usually seems to fall. But the change in pitch is not a feature that is random or inevitable – people can make their voices rise at the end of an utterance if they want to. Intonation is part of a system where choices are made by speakers to convey different meanings. As in any linguistic system, speakers can produce particular forms, and recognize those forms when other speakers produce them. So it is with intonation, speakers select high, low, rising, falling, and so on to convey contrasts of meaning.

When a person hears an unfamiliar language or accent, their attention is often drawn to the intonation patterns, and they will say the language is 'sing-song', 'lilting', 'flat' or even 'monotone'. What this shows is that they are hearing intonation patterns that are different from the ones they are used to in their own accent or language.

Analysing the basic tones

Exercise 1

In the interaction between grandmother and grandson, try to identify the pitch changes. To begin with, listen for the basic contrast between rise and fall. Mark rising pitch with an upward pointing arrow ↗ and falling pitch with a downward arrow ↘. Use a combination of both arrows to mark any tones which seem to rise and then start to fall ∧ or fall then rise ∨. Put the arrows in front of the syllable or word where you hear the pitch movement most clearly.

The child has a lot of patience with his grandmother – there are over a dozen similar exchanges based on her misnamings. Another adult would probably have told her she was being silly early on when she calls a car a big red ball. The pattern of these exchanges goes something like this: she turns a page, makes a (false) statement about the objects in the picture, the child then recognizes her 'mistake' and contradicts or corrects her. She then restates her label, and then the child contradicts her again. She then says 'oh' or 'ok', accepting his label for the objects, and carries on.

Exercise 2

Keeping in mind the above pattern of the exchanges, answer the following questions about choice of tone.

Question 1

What type of tone do the speakers use when they are stating, restating and contradicting – falling or rising?

Question 2

The child usually begins his contradiction with the word 'no'. What tones does he use on this word?

Question 3

When the grandmother accepts his correction, what tone does she use on the words 'oh ok'.

Question 4

When his grandmother seems to accept his name for the object, by using it herself, as in 'they're balls' (line 23) and 'they're butterflies' (line 45), he responds with the word 'yeah'. What tone does he use?

Given the usage highlighted in questions 1–4 above, what generalization could be made about choice of tone made by speakers when they are stating, restating, contradicting, and so on?

Listen again to lines 5 to 7. On this occasion the child contradicts his grandmother, and then, because she persists in her naming, he contradicts her again. Notice that the tone he uses on the second contradiction is different from that used on the first. On the re-contradiction, his pitch is higher at the beginning of the pitch movement.

Exercise 3

Question 1

Look for other examples of the child's contradictions where you hear him use high pitch. Mark these in the transcript with 'H'.

How might this contrast between what seem to be two types of contradictions – one with a shift up to high pitch, and one without, be explained? Try to consider this in terms of the child's aims or goals in communicating with his grandmother.

Question 2

Look for examples in the grandmother's utterances where she also seems to be using falling tones that begin on a high pitch, and falling tones which have a lower pitch as their starting point. Mark the pattern with high-pitch onset with an 'H' in the transcript. Do grandmother and child share the same system? In other words, are they making a choice between these two types of falling tone for the same reason?

Exercise 4

Identify the occasions where the grandmother uses a rising intonation pattern that finishes on a high pitch in her normal speaking range. Think of 'high pitch' and 'normal' in the following way – if her voice went any higher it would sound very tense or 'screechy'. It would have a distinctive quality. Sometimes this type of ultra-high pitch is represented as 'eek' in comics or stories. In other words, a speaker, because of fear or surprise, moves beyond the pitch height of their normal speaking range. So we are using 'high' here to describe the top of the speaker's *normal* pitch range.

Mark these high-rising tones with the letters 'HT', for 'high terminal' – finishing at a high point – in the transcript.

Fall-rise tones and level tones

There are two types of tone that the speakers use that we haven't yet focused on. The first is the tone used by the grandmother when she is about to misname. If you listen to lines 8 and 19 as she says 'I think they are . . .' you'll hear that the word 'are' is stretched out. However, there doesn't seem to be an change of pitch direction, either falling or rising. We can call this type of tone a 'level tone'.

The second is exemplified by the child. When he says 'you're being silly' (line 57), notice that both 'being' and 'silly' have a tone which rises before it falls. Compare the word 'silly' here with the first time he uses it at line 33. When he says 'you're silly' at line 33, he uses a simple falling tone. Other examples of this rise-fall used by the child are at line 22 on 'no' and line 24 on 'yeah'. The grandmother uses it at line 36 on the word 'oh'. In discussions of the meaning of tones, this has been described as an emphatic type of falling tone.

The child's pronunciation of words

The words in this conversation with grandmother are words for common objects; many of these words will have been part of the child's vocabulary for a while, and his grandmother understands him well.

Exercise 5

Listen again to his pronunciation of the following words. Compare his pronunciation with that of his grandmother when she says the same word before or after him. Show any differences between their pronunciations by transcribing them.

Line	Word	Child	Grandmother
9/10	apples		
11/12	tomatoes		
22/23	balls		
29/30	ice creams		
44/45	butterflies		
53/54	strawberries		

Tasks for discussion or consolidation

Make a recording of a child of about the same age talking to an adult. Choose an everyday activity like this one. Try to transcribe and analyse the intonation patterns used by adult and child.

Looking back

In this unit we have examined the basic elements of intonation. We have identified some of the choices speakers make in their use of tones or pitch movements, and considered some possible meanings. We have also looked at how relative pitch height is used, and how speakers can begin a pitch movement at different points in their pitch range. We have begun to explore intonation as a linguistic system, and in doing so, have seen how a child of two years and eight months has control of that system and uses it to communicate meaning.

We have introduced one of the conventions used to represent intonation patterns, e.g. directional arrows.

Even in this superficially simple interaction, we have seen how complex the use of intonation can be, and how difficult it is to analyse. But despite this, it is important to consider the use of intonation in real interactions rather than looking at a line of print and trying to imagine how it would be said, i.e. trying to hear it 'in your head'.

Unit 4 Key and comments

Exercise 1

Note: treat this first version as a working draft. We will be adding to it as we progress.

      C: \a car
      G: it's a big red\ball
      C: Vno a\car
      G: \oh\ok   I think that's two\dogs
5   **C:** Vno\ducks
      G: two\dogs
      C: no\ducks
      G: \ducks   oh\ok   how about\those I think they are \bananas
      C: Vno are\apples
10 **G:** \apples   they're↗apples
      C: um   um um\tomatoes
      G: oh they're↗tomatoes   well they\do look likeVtomatoes \don't they
      C: \yeah
      G: they are\cars
15 **C:** Vno are\boats
      G: they're\cars
      C: no they\boats
      G: \oh I'm sorry   I'm not very\good at\this\ok they are
         I\think they are\trucks
20 **C:** Vno are\balls
      G: there's five\trucks there
      C: ∧no are\balls
      G: they're\balls

    C: /\yeah

25 **G:** \oh let me see if I can do better on this\one
       these are little\boys

    C: V no are ice\creams

    G: they're little\boys

    C: no are ice\creams

30 **G:** they're ice V creams

    C: \yeah

    G: \oh\ok

    C: you're\silly

    G: I'm/what   I'm/silly

35 **C:** \yeah

    G: /\oh that's not very\nice is it   ok these are\books

    C: V no they're\lollipops

    G: one two three four five six seven\books

    C: V no V no are\apples

40 **G:** they're\apples now are/they   they're\apples I think they're\books

    C: no they're\not   they're\not   'cause are lollipops

    G: oh ok I'll take your\word for it now/\these are one two
       three four five six seven eight little\girls

    C: V no are\butterflies

45 **G:** they're/butterflies

    C: \yeah

    G: you/\sure

    C: \yeah

    G: \oh\ok

50 **C:** you're being\silly

    G: I'm being very\silly   now these are one two three
       four five six seven eight nine\apples

    C: V no are\strawberries

    G: they're/strawberries

55 **C:** \yeah

    G: how do you know they're\strawberries

    C: you're/\being/\silly

    G: I'm a very silly\grandma I\know

    C: you you don't\know

60 **G:** I don't know\what

    C: you don't know the\words

EXERCISE 2   Question 1

Falling tones are used by both speakers.

EXERCISE 2   Question 2

The tone he uses most frequently is a fall-rise. At line 41, where he is saying 'no they're not', he uses a fall.

EXERCISE 2   Question 3

She uses a fall. At line 18, where she says 'oh' and then seems to apologize ('I'm sorry') she also uses a falling tone.

EXERCISE 2   Question 4

He uses falling tones on 'yeah'.

Falling tones seem to be used for the speech functions of stating, restating and contradicting. This tone is also used when the child confirms a name or agrees with his grandmother, as for example at lines 30/31, 'G: they're ice creams; C: yeah', or at lines 12/13, 'G: they do look like tomatoes don't they; C: yeah'.

We might say that what these utterances all have in common is that the speaker is stating or asserting, or telling the other speaker something. See PE5 11.6.2.3, where this tone is described as 'matter-of-fact' and 'assertive'. The label 'proclaiming tone' has also been used (Brazil (1994)). Kreidler (1997: 181) says this tone is used 'when you have something to tell someone, you say it, you have no intention of saying anything more, (and) you don't mean to imply more than you have said'.

When the child says 'no' before his contradictions, he uses a fall-rise. This choice could be said to show 'continuation'. That is, the word 'no' precedes the next part of his utterance which provides the right name, as at line 5 'Vno\ducks'. PE5 says that the fall-rise is 'continuative and non-assertive' (p. 243). Roach (1991: 138) says that 'in a variety of ways, this tone conveys an impression that something more is to follow'.

EXERCISE 3   Questions 1 and 2

The falls beginning on a high pitch, sometimes called 'high falls', occur at the following lines:

3 no a car;   7 no ducks;   9 no are apples;   20 no are balls;
39 no no are apples;   44 no are butterflies.

When the speakers use these high falls, they seem to be a stronger version of the simple fall. Kreidler (1997: 184) refers to them as a 'more dynamic or dramatic equivalent'. We could also say that the main element of meaning is that of *contrast* – what you are saying is in contrast to what I am saying. So, from the child's perspective, when his grandmother continues to get the names wrong, he wants to be more forceful and assertive in his correction of her, so he chooses extra pitch height, high onset, in other words, a 'stronger' version of the falling tone.

If we restrict our analysis to this particular context – stating the names of the pictures, contradicting, restating, then accepting someone else's claim, then both grandmother and grandson seem to be using the same system.

EXERCISE 4

Rises which finish on a high pitch, sometimes called a 'high rise' are used at the following lines:

10 they're apples
34 I'm what   I'm silly
45 they're butterflies
54 they're strawberries

In each of these the speaker seems to be asking a question. In 'I'm what' this is confirmed by the grammar – 'I'm what' is the equivalent of 'What am I?' or 'What did you say I am?' In particular, we could say that these are 'echo questions' because the speaker echoes the words of the previous speaker.

Rising tones are often used when asking for repetition or clarification of something that has been said. They are therefore 'continuative' because something more is expected. The term 'non-final' has also been used. We could also think of rising tones as being oriented towards the person addressed. The speaker is waiting to hear from the addressee (Kreidler 1997: 185). We might also say that in this context, the grandmother is pretending to be surprised, and surprise seems to be conveyed by rising tones which finish high. (See PE 5 11.6.2.3.)

EXERCISE 5

Line	Word	Child	Grandmother
9/10	apples	apəlz	apəlz
11/12	tomatoes	təmɑtoʊz	təmɑtoʊz
22/23	balls	bɔːlz	bɔːlz
29/30	ice creams	aɪs kiːmz	aɪs kriːmz
44/45	butterflies	bʌtəfwaɪz	bʌtəflaɪz
53/54	strawberries	sɔbiz	strɔːbriz

Alternating rhythm

Preview

The rhythm of a language is one of its fundamental features. The word 'rhythm' comes from Greek 'rhythmus' which means 'flow'. Rhythm is the sense of movement in speech. We will use several types of texts read aloud and excerpts from a rehearsal of a drama group to investigate the rhythm of English.

Background

In some styles of speaking the rhythm appears more obvious or marked than usual. One example is when speakers deliver an oath, e.g. the pledge of allegiance to the flag on formal occasions in United States. Another example is the recitation of parts of the liturgy used in religious services. A further example is the reading aloud of poetry. The flow or sense of movement of the lines of a poem is controlled and manipulated by poets. There are also dramatists who exert the same kind of control in their plays. We will use recordings of some poems in English, including some derived versions of these poems, to analyse English rhythm. Recordings of a rehearsal session for a performance at a drama festival will also be used to reveal some of the factors actors consider when they are deciding how to deliver written lines in a script.

What is the rhythm of English based on?

When we speak, there seems to be more energy involved in producing some syllables than in others, and when we listen to others speaking we recognize that some of the syllables are more prominent than others. The syllables that we hear as more prominent are said to be **stressed**. There seem to be four features involved in this perception of prominence:

(a) most people seem to feel that stressed syllables are louder than unstressed.

(b) the length of a syllable has an important part to play in its prominence. For example, if the vowel in a syllable is held longer before it is 'cut off' by a following consonant sound, then that syllable will be heard as prominent.

(c) **pitch** The vocal cords can vibrate at different speeds. If there is a change of speed on a particular syllable, either faster (resulting in a higher pitch) or slower (resulting in a lower pitch) or some fluctuations in speed, then this syllable will stand out from the others around it if they don't have any or as much variation in pitch.

(d) a syllable will be heard as stressed if it has a vowel that differs in quality from the others around it. For example, if you repeat the syllable /dɪ/ several times to imitate the firing of a machine gun or the sound of someone tapping [dɪdɪdɪdɪ], and then change the vowel in the last syllable to [a], as in [dɪdɪdɪda], that last syllable will seem to stand out from the others. The same will happen if you put [a] in the second, third, etc., syllable and say [dɪdɪda dɪdɪ]. We can view stressed syllables as occurring against a background of unstressed syllables.

So in answer to the question: 'what is the rhythm of English based on?', we could say that it is based on differences in energy, which seems to contribute to a foregrounding of some syllables. In the stream or flow of speech, there is an alternation of syllables which seem to be prominent with those that are not so prominent, that is, an alternation of stressed and unstressed syllables.

Exercise 1

Listen to the recording of the first two stanzas of the following poem and try to decide which of the syllables in each line are stressed and which are not. Mark the ones you hear as more prominent than others in some way, e.g. by underlining them.

Sequence I

Elegy written in a Country Churchyard
THOMAS GRAY

The curfew tolls the knell of parting day,
The lowing herd winds slowly o'er the lea,
The ploughman homeward plods his weary way,
And leaves the world to darkness and to me.

Now fades the glimmering landscape on the sight,
And all the air a solemn stillness holds,
Save where the beetle wheels his droning flight,
And drowsy tinklings lull the distant folds . . .

What type of rhythm does English have?

English has been classified as a language which uses **stress-timing**, that is, its timing is based on stressed syllables that occur at approximately regular intervals in the stream of speech. In order to create this sense of a regular pulse, like a heart beat, other syllables, the unstressed ones, can be compressed or reduced in some way. For example, the consonants in the syllables are deleted, or the vowel at the core of the unstressed syllables will be pronounced as schwa, or as /ɪ/, or as a short version of a vowel in the area of /ʊ/. (These have been termed **weak syllables** and the vowels in their nucleus are called **weak vowels**.)

This phenomenon is sometimes represented in writing by spellings such as 'bread'n butter' for 'bread and butter' or 'cuppa' for 'cup of coffee/tea'.

In analysing stress-timing, we use the unit of rhythm known as the **foot**. Each foot will have one stressed syllable; if a foot has other *un*stressed syllables, they can undergo compression and weakening. If a foot has only the one stressed syllable, then it may be lengthened to maintain the steady rhythm. So, according to this view, there are five feet in the first line of the poem.

Other languages have been classified as being 'syllable-timed'. It has been claimed that in this type of rhythm, timing is based upon the syllable. But this is not to say that there is no difference between syllables. For example, some syllables may have a shorter vowel than others in a syllable-timed rhythm. There is somehow a different sense of movement or flow in syllable-timing.

Exercise 2

Question 1

Listen to Sequences 2 and 3. These are two versions of Gray's *Elegy*. They were devised by Professor H. G. Widdowson for his book on the study of poetry, *Practical Stylistics*. Try to hear the beat of stressed syllables in both readings, and then compare the lines in these versions in terms of the pattern of stressed and unstressed syllables. Try to identify any other differences you hear in the rhythm of the original and the derived versions.

Sequence 2

Version 1

> The curfew tolls the knell of parting day,
> The herd is winding slowly o'er the lea,
> The ploughman is plodding on his weary way,
> Leaving the world to darkness and to me.
>
> The landscape now is fading on the sight,
> And all the air a solemn stillness holds,
> Save for the beetle wheeling in his flight,
> And drowsy tinklings lulling distant folds . . .

Sequence 3

Version 2

> The curfew ends the day,
> The herd winds o'er the lea,
> The ploughman plods his way,
> And leaves the world to me.
>
> The landscape fades on the sight,
> The air a stillness holds,
> Save for the beetle's flight,
> And tinklings in the folds . . .

In the analysis of poetry, the notion of the 'foot' is also used. There are various metrical conventions that have been used by poets writing in English. Sometimes only the number of stressed syllables per foot is controlled, and the number of unstressed is not fixed. Sometimes the number of unstressed syllables is also fixed.

A continuum rather than two types of rhythm

These two categories of rhythm in languages may be useful in drawing attention to some important rhythmic characteristics, but a language cannot be strictly categorized as fitting into one or the other. It is very important to remember that stress-timing is a *tendency* in English. The timing of stressed syllables at regular intervals is not uniform throughout speech. There are two key characteristics of the rhythm of English: one is the *alternation* of stressed and unstressed, or 'strong' and 'weak' syllables, and the second is that in English, as opposed to other languages, the difference between strong and weak syllables is quite extreme.

Perhaps we could make a comparison between a photograph where the objects in the foreground are very brightly lit, and those in the background are very dimly lit and hardly visible, and another photograph in which objects in the foreground stand out, but the contrast with those in the background is not so strong. The photograph with strong lighting contrasts is analogous to English rhythm, the photograph with less extreme differences is analogous to languages that we would place on the syllable-timed part of the continuum, such as Spanish or Japanese.

Exercise 3

A useful illustration of how rhythmic features are emphasized and exploited for effect by poets is a comparison of a poem and a prose version derived from it. The poem is *This is Just to Say* by William Carlos Williams. The derived version takes the form of a note, quickly written on a scrap of paper, and left perhaps on a kitchen table.

S e q u e n c e   4

(You will hear two different readers.)

> *This is Just to Say*
>
> I have eaten
> the plums
> that were in
> the icebox
>
> and which
> you were probably
> saving
> for breakfast
>
> Forgive me
> they were delicious
> so sweet
> and so cold

Prose version: This is just to say that I have eaten the plums that were in the icebox. They were delicious, so sweet and so cold. But you were probably saving them for breakfast. Forgive me.

Question 1

How do the readers seem to respond to the structure of the lines in the poem in terms of their use of stress and pauses?

Question 2

Devise another version of the note, which is even more brief. (Imagine what you would write if you had eaten these plums and were hurrying out of the house but wanted to leave a quick note.) What words would you decide to retain and which would you leave out?

Question 3

Here are two versions of a poem by Robert Graves and the original. Analyse how the rhythm of the lines varies. What effects does the layout of lines in Text C seem to have on the reader in terms of his use of pauses and stress/unstress?

Sequence 5

Text A (original)

Flying Crooked

The butterfly, a cabbage-white,
(His honest idiocy of flight)
Will never now, it is too late,
Master the art of flying straight,
Yet has – who knows so well as I? –
A just sense of how not to fly:
He lurches here and here by guess
And God and hope and hopelessness.
Even the aerobatic swift
Has not his flying-crooked gift.

Text B

I watched a butterfly, a cabbage white,
Lurching across a field in crooked flight.
I watched it pass and thought: it is too late
For it to learn the art of flying straight,
The deft direction-finding of the swift.
Yet flying crooked also is a gift.

Text C

         does not fly
The butterfly   straight;
It finds   by hope and
    its way   fate.
             gift
But flying   a
    crooked is
Denied the aerobatic swift.
I recognize   mine,
    this gift as
  predictably
Un   off-
         line.

Exercise 4

Tam O'Shanter

The next poem is one of the most famous ever written in Scots, Tam O'Shanter, by Robert Burns (1759–96). Burns is the national poet of Scotland. In his poetry, he draws upon various styles, such as folk-song, storytelling, preaching, and the language of everyday conversation. This poem tells the story of what happened to Tam (Tom) O'Shanter as he rode home one night through a storm after drinking and carousing in the local pub with his friend Souter Johnny. The poem has a very strong, regular rhythm.

Sequence 6

(The meanings of words that might not be familiar, either because they are typically Scots, or from the eighteenth century, are given below the stanzas.)

Below is the first stanza of Tam O'Shanter:

> When chapman billies leave the street,
> And drouthy neebors, neebors meet,
> As market-days are wearing late,
> An' folk begin to tak the gate;
> While we sit bousing at the nappy,
> An' getting fou and unco happy,
> We think na on the lang Scots miles,
> The mosses, waters, slaps, and styles,
> That lie between us and our hame,
> Whare sits our sulky sullen dame,
> Gathering her brows like gathering storm,
> Nursing her wrath to keep it warm.

(chapman billies: packman fellows/ drouthy: thirsty/ tak the gate: take to the road; start for home/ bousing: drinking/ nappy: ale/ fou: drunk/ unco: very/ na: no/ lang: long/ slaps and styles: gaps in a wall or fence/ hame: home)

Question 1

The rhythm of the first four lines of this stanza are identical. What pattern do they have?

Question 2

The last two lines of stanza one have four stresses, but the arrangement of stressed and unstressed syllables is different from the other lines in the stanza. How does it differ?

Question 3

There is one line that ends with three stressed syllables with no unstressed ones in between – which is it?

(Stanzas two and three are about how husbands always fail to take the advice given to them by their wives.) Here are stanzas four and five:

> Ah, gentle dames! it gars me greet,
> To think how mony counsels sweet,
> How mony lengthen'd sage advices,
> The husband frae the wife despises!
>
> But to our tale: Ae market-night,
> Tam had got planted unco right;
> Fast by an ingle, bleezing finely,
> Wi' reaming swats, that drank divinely;
> And at his elbow, Souter Johnny,
> His ancient, trusty, drouthy crony;
> Tam lo'ed him like a vera brither;
> They had been fou for weeks thegither.
> The night drave on wi' sangs and clatter;
> And ay the ale was growing better:
> The landlady and Tam grew gracious,
> Wi' favours, secret, sweet, and precious:
> The Souter tauld his queerest stories;
> The landlord's laugh was ready chorus:
> The storm without might rair and rustle,
> Tam did na mind the storm a whistle.

(gars me greet: it makes me weep/ mony: many/ frae: from/ ae: one/ planted: settled/ ingle: corner/ reaming swats: frothing ale/ souter: cobbler/ vera: very/ brither: brother/ thegither: together/ sangs: songs/ ay: always/ tauld: told/ rair: roar)

Question 4

Do any of the lines break the pattern of four stressed syllables?

Question 5

One of the lines has the pattern: – / – – – / / / – (where / stands for a stress and – an unstressed syllable). Which is it?

Question 6

Of the candidates for stresses in line 5 of the fifth stanza, ELbow, SOUter, and JOHNny are the obvious candidates. But this would result in only three stresses; which word does the reader select to receive the fourth stress?

Exercise 5

These sequences come from a recording of a drama group rehearsing a performance of a play based on the legends of King Arthur, Camelot and the Knights of the Round Table. Like many of these myths and stories, this story revolves around a curse or spell cast on an innocent person, who is then saved by a noble person who makes a sacrifice. In this story a beautiful young woman, Dame Ragnell, has been turned into an ugly old woman. The good and noble person is Sir Gawain, one of King Arthur's knights, who breaks the spell by agreeing to marry her in order to save the king from being killed by a vengeful knight.

The story opens with King Arthur hunting deer; he meets a 'strange knight', Gromer, who threatens to kill him. In order to save his own life, Arthur promises to give the knight anything he wishes.

Sequence 7

Narrator 1 Listen
In the time of Arthur, courteous and royal,
Who of all kings was the flower,
And of knighthood bore the honour,
Was nothing but chivalry,
And the brave were loved and cowards disgraced.

Narrator 2 Now Arthur was hunting in Ingleswood,
and all his knights were there beside.
When from a stand a deer did run.

Arthur	Hold still every man, I will slay it, if I can. The King stalks that deer . . .

(In chasing the deer, Arthur comes upon Gromer)

Gromer	Well met Arthur! You have wronged me many a year. So woefully I shall quit you here. The days of your life are done.

(Arthur bargains for his life by promising to do anything Gromer asks.)

Arthur	Yes, lo, here is my hand.

Gromer	Wait, and listen first, Sir King, You shall swear upon my sword To tell me, here, alone at twelve months' end, What women desire most. And if you bring no answer, without fail, Your head you lose. What say you, Sir King?

Arthur	I agree, now let me go.

Gromer	Keep this secret, trick me in no way, Or, by Mary mild, your life you lose.

Question 1

Because of the slightly archaic English used, there are several lines, or parts of lines, which have a series of stressed syllables with no unstressed syllables in between them. In other words, these lines have what sounds like syllable-timing instead of stress-timing. Find some examples of lines with this rhythm.

Question 2

Two of the longest lines in these excerpts are the first and last lines spoken by Narrator 1. How would you analyse them in terms of stressed and unstressed syllables?

Sequence 7 (continued)

In the following extracts we see Arthur returning to Camelot, where he seeks the help of Sir Gawain, who comes up with a plan.

Gawain	Ye, Sir, make good cheer.
	Ride throughout the land
	Ask every woman and man,
	What women desire most,
	I will go another way,
	And every answer I shall write down.

Narrator 1	The King rode one way, Gawain the other,
	And everywhere they asked
	What women desired most.

Narrator 2	Some said they most loved riches,
	Some said to be well arrayed,
	Some to be flattered and well-praised,
	Some said a lusty man
	That in their arms they could embrace,
	Some said one thing, some another,
	No two could agree together.

Question 3

When the actor says the words 'some said' does she always deliver them in the same way?

In the next excerpt Arthur meets an old ugly woman, Dame Ragnell, on his search, who tells him she can help him.

Narrator 1	King Arthur rode into Ingleswood
	And, between oak and green holly,
	Came upon a creature so ungodly,
	He marvelled.
. . .	
Ragnell	God speed, Sir King.
	Speak with me before you go –
	Your life is in my hands.

| Arthur | What would you with me? |

Ragnell	Of all the answers you can yelp
	Not one of them will be any help.
	If I help you not, you are dead.
	Grant me, Sir King, but one thing,
	And your life I guarantee

Or else . . .
You must grant me Gawain to wed –
And through my answer your life be saved.
Grant me to be Gawain's wife,
It must be so, or you are dead.
Choose, or soon you lose you head.

Question 4

In the speeches of Dame Ragnell, the actor chooses to make particular words prominent. Which words does she select, and why do you think she has chosen these words?

As part of their rehearsal, the actors discuss various lines in the script and how they should be delivered.

Exercise 6

Listen to these extracts from their discussion, and identify the features of rhythm and stress that they appeal to in their decisions about their performance. The first extract concerns three lines spoken by the Narrator 1 which are printed in their script as follows:

And forth they rode, though Arthur grieved
Side by side, it liked the king full ill.
And the company in the court had wonder.

In modern English the meaning intended is: They (Arthur and Dame Ragnell) rode off side by side. The king did not like this at all, and the people in the court were amazed and puzzled.

Sequence 8

A: . . . on page six + third speech down narrator one + um there was a thing of + the middle line + (unintell) and forth they rode + though Arthur grieved + side by side + I thought the emphasis ought ought to be on 'it' + it liked the king full well full ill I mean it's the situation that he didn't . . . [they read it to themselves] it liked the king full ill + D: no I think 'liked' B: it's very unnatural to me David A: no no that suggests 'it liked' the king really this is a negative isn't it + the king liked it full ill . . . C: well I think if you're going to put the stress there and I can see the argument for it it shouldn't be the word 'it' it should be 'this' or something like that + this liked the king full well B: that's good C: that liked the king full well C: to stress 'it' seems somehow wrong A: 'this' then suggests it's the 'side by side' it's the situation the king doesn't like in general C: 'this' can be the general situation couldn't it A: following straight upon 'side by side' it C: it really does seem rather funny to stress 'it' D: I still think it's 'it' but the emphasis is on the 'liked' C: yes I would agree with David D: and forth they rode though Arthur grieved side by side + it liked the king full ill + C: this liked the king full ill D: and the company and the court had wonder C: yes I can't see any reason to + emphasise 'it' A: he didn't like it C: I think what we need is a full stop after 'side' isn't it + side by side + and forth they rode though Arthur grieved + side by side + full stop + this or it + liked the king full ill (B: yes) full stop . . .

E: . . . going back to page + page three + narrator one the middle speech and Arthur rode into Ingleswood King Arthur rode into Ingleswood (A: yes) I think we might take out the 'king' + Arthur rode into Ingleswood C: no I think you're losing rhythm there Pete if you take these words out 'Arthur rode into Ingleswood King Arthur rode into Ingleswood' C: it's rather like the pause for the time lapse + a new scene if there were the tiniest more pause there + it would separate the scenes B: that's it that's the answer C: so you get . . . yes it's like the way we marked it before . . . about you know they retired as it were A: day breaks C: the meal done and they retire . . . B: it it gives a sort of riding rhythm . . .

[Their next discussion centres on the very first line of the play.]

. . . C: there's one line Arthur when Arthur's first mentioned it seemed to me + it should be stressed in the same way + Eileen did it when she was Narrator two but I think even more 'in the time of Arthur' . . . (yes . . . that's right) so that we can all glory in the word B: telling just when it happened yes C: because again I think you were just saying about attention it must be up + attention catching B: yes this is about Arthur C: yes . . .

Looking back

In this unit we have used readings aloud to examine the typical rhythm of English, and to explore the production and perception of the phenomenon of prominence. We have used the rehearsal process of a group of actors to demonstrate how speakers can manipulate stress and rhythm, and to reveal how they think it contributes to the effect of their speech on the listener.

Tasks for discussion or consolidation

Choose any of the poems in the unit and record yourself reading them aloud. Compare your readings with those in the recordings in terms of rhythm.

Select a poem you know well and try to write your own modified or derived version, manipulating the number of stresses in a particular line or the number of unstressed syllables.

Examine some examples of strongly rhythmical texts, for example, children's skipping rhymes, or catch phrases, or proverbs. Analyse their rhythm and investigate whether certain rhythmic patterns seem to recur in the same type of text.

Unit 5 Key and comments

EXERCISE 1

Stressed syllables are shown by upper case.

> The CURfew TOLLS the KNELL of PARTing DAY,
> The LOWing HERD WINDS SLOWly O'ER the LEA,
> The PLOUGHman HOMEward PLODS his WEARY WAY,
> And LEAVES the WORLD to DARKness AND to ME.
>
> NOW FADES the GLIMmering LANDscape on the SIGHT,
> And ALL the AIR a SOLemn STILLness HOLDS,
> SAVE where the BEEtle WHEELS his DRONing FLIGHT,
> And DROWsy TINKlings LULL the DIStant FOLDS . . .

The alternation of stressed and unstressed syllables is very regular in this poem. Each line has five stressed syllables, or beats. The one exception is line 2 where the reader uses six. Notice that in line 2 there is a succession of three stressed syllables with no intervening unstressed one: HERD WINDS SLOWly. This seems to slow down the pace, perhaps to imitate the slow movement of the cattle, and perhaps leads to the word 'o'er' being stressed. The steady alternation of one stressed followed by one unstressed syllable returns in lines 3 and 4, and seems to result in the word 'and' receiving a stress. This contrasts with the following pattern: And LEAVES the WORLD to DARKness and to ME, which one might have expected. The beat falling on 'and' perhaps reinforces the poet's intention to focus on the sense of aloneness that the narrator of the poem is feeling.

EXERCISE 2 Question 1

VERSION 1

> The CURfew TOLLS the KNELL of PARTing DAY,
> The HERD is WINDing SLOWly O'ER the LEA,
> The PLOUGHman is PLODding on his WEARY WAY,
> LEAVing the WORLD to DARKness AND to ME.
>
> The LANDscape NOW is FADing on the SIGHT,
> And ALL the AIR a SOLemn STILLness HOLDS,
> SAVE for the BEEtle WHEELing in his FLIGHT,
> And DROWsy TINKlings LULLing DIStant FOLDS . . .

VERSION 2

> The CURfew ENDS the DAY,
> The HERD WINDS o'er the LEA,
> The PLOUGHman PLODS his WAY,
> And LEAVES the WORLD to ME.
>
> The LANDscape FADES on the SIGHT,
> The AIR a STILLness HOLDS,
> SAVE for the BEEtle's FLIGHT,
> And TINKlings IN the FOLDS . . .

Version 1 also shows a regular alternation of five stressed syllables with unstressed ones in-between. Although the number of unstressed syllables varies, for example line 3 has seven unstressed syllables, while lines 1 and 4 have five, the overall impression is that these lines are 'equal' in length.

Version 2 has a pattern of three stressed syllables or beats. There is less variation in the number of unstressed syllables. Lines 5 and 7 have a sequence of two unstressed syllables between stressed ones: FADES on the SIGHT and SAVE for the BEEtle's. Notice how these are pronounced in a way that seems to maintain the steady progression of strong stresses.

Note that in the original poem each line of stanza one begins with an unstressed syllable. Stanza two departs from this, in that lines 5 and 7 begin with stressed syllables. We see the same kind of variation in Version 1. In the first stanza the first three lines all begin with unstressed syllables, but the fourth begins with 'leaving' which must have a stress on the first syllable. Perhaps writers in English realize that if lines are too repetitive in terms of rhythm the effect will lull the reader or listener into drowsiness.

EXERCISE 3 Question 1

When the phrase 'this is just to say' is read as the title of the poem, it is given three stressed syllables: THIS is JUST to SAY. When read as the beginning of the note, the word 'this' does not receive a stress. The choice of syllables to be stressed is very similar in the poem readings and in the note reading: the following words are stressed in both by the readers: EATen, PLUMS, ICEbox, PROBably, SAVing BREAKfast.

There is some variation in the pronunciation of the phrase 'they were delicious'. The female reader chooses to put stress on the first two words as well as on the second syllable of 'delicious', whereas the male reader puts the stress or prominence only 'deLICious'. The phrase 'so sweet and so cold' seems to offer a range of choices. In the prose reading the second occurrence of 'so' receives a stress, but in both poem readings the prominence seems to be on the adjectives 'sweet and cold'. Perhaps their position at the end of the poetic line has led to this.

EXERCISE 3 Question 2

Here is a possible additional version of the note:

ate the plums in the icebox   really delicious – so sweet & cold   guess you were saving them for breakfast   sorry

EXERCISE 3 Question 3

Both the original and Version 1 share a regular alternation of stressed and unstressed syllables. The pattern could be represented with a – mark for unstressed and a / mark for stressed. If all the lines are marked this way in both Texts A and B then the pattern with four stresses seems to be the basic template: – / – / – / – /, with a few variations. Note that there is also a consistency in the way a line finishes. The last syllable is always stressed. The layout of Text C seems to promote the use of pauses, which gives a jerkiness to the reading, imitating perhaps the physical characteristics of the flight of the butterfly. The only exception to this is the line which is written on only one line: Denied the aerobatic swift. This receives the following steady rhythm: – / – / – / – /.

We have been focusing on the syllables or words which are stressed in these poems, but there seems to be another aspect to the stress patterns of English, especially poetry. At the end of each line there seems to be a beat without a syllable. This phenomenon is known as 'silent stress'.

EXERCISE 3 **Question 4**

The reader of Text A does not use a silent stress between the seventh and the eighth lines but carries the phrasing over from the word 'guess' to 'and God . . .'.

EXERCISE 4 **Question 1**

Using / for a stressed and – for an unstressed syllable, the pattern is – / – / – / – / .

EXERCISE 4 **Question 2**

/ – – – / – / – – /

EXERCISE 4 **Question 3**

We think na on the lang Scots miles,

(Note that in Lowland Scots the word 'lang' would be pronounced as [laŋ] not [lɔːŋ].)

EXERCISE 4 **Question 4**

But TO our TALE: AE MARket NIGHT.

EXERCISE 4 **Question 5**

The LANDlady and TAM GREW GRAcious.

EXERCISE 4 **Question 6**

The first word of the line – 'and'.

EXERCISE 5 **Question 1**

These lines seem to be a series of stressed monosyllables so they could be said to resemble syllable-timing:

> I will slay it, if I can.
> Your head you lose.
> What say you, Sir King?

and the following parts of lines:

> . . . now let me go.
> . . . your life you lose.

Question 2

IN the TIME of ARthur COURteous and ROYal
And the BRAVE were LOVED and COwards disGRACED

Question 3

The placement of stress is consistent throughout; both words are stressed.

Question 4

<u>Your</u> life is in <u>my</u> hands.

There seems to be a strong contrast or opposition set up between 'your' and 'my'.

Not one of them will be <u>any</u> help.

Here the meaning seems to be 'absolutely none at all'.

You must grant me <u>Gawain</u> to wed. Only Gawain will do, none other.

It <u>must</u> be <u>so</u>. There is no choice.

In discussing whether 'it' should be stressed, the actors appeal to the tendency in English for pronouns (he/she/it/they, etc.) not to be stressed, because they usually refer to people or things that have already been mentioned. One of the actors thinks it would be 'unnatural' and 'funny' if 'it' were stressed, indicating that for such a word to be stressed would break a pattern or expectation. However, substituting the word 'this' and stressing that word: '<u>this</u> liked the 'king' could be done because it would set up a contrast – he might have liked something else, but not 'this'.

When C suggests the need for a 'full stop' instead of a comma she seems to be referring to the need for a 'silent stress' or 'beat' in the reading.

In the discussion about whether the word 'King' can be taken out, two of the actors seem to feel that even removing a word of one syllable can lead to a 'loss' of rhythm. As it stands, the pattern seems to be: King ARthur RODE into INGlesWOOD, and, as one actor comments, this pattern imitates the rhythm of riding a horse, so the meaning of the words and the rhythm of the line are linked.

In discussing the way the name 'Arthur' should be said, the actors show that they think one purpose of stress is to call the audience's attention to a word. In the first line of the play, the naming of 'Arthur' will give a great deal of information to the listeners – the subject, the time, the setting and perhaps even the theme. This case is a good example of not only the stressing of particular syllable as part of the typical rhythm of English, but of the role of foregrounding – making something prominent. Notice, that the actor's proposed delivery of the word 'Arthur' really involves a lot of pitch change.

'can you imagine . . .'

Preview

We will be analysing extracts from a sermon delivered as part of a religious service. Our main focus will be on the fact that each English word of two syllables or more has a distinct pattern or 'shape'. This 'shape' is based on the relationship between the syllables – some syllables in English words stand out from the others. As we saw in Unit 5, listeners can recognize which syllable is more 'prominent' than the others, and speakers pronounce prominent and non-prominent syllables in different ways. A syllable which stands out is said to be 'stressed' or 'accented'. We will also look at the variation in pronunciation of some common words. Another focus will be intonation.

Background

The speaker, who is a middle-aged male from the London area, belongs to the Jehovah's Witnesses, a society of Christians organized in the 1870s by Charles Russell. Their religious meetings are held in 'Kingdom Halls'. In this sect there is an emphasis on Bible study, and at several points in the sermon, the speaker refers the members of the congregation to verses in the Bible, which he then reads aloud to them as they read along in their own Bibles. At some points you can hear the rustling sound of pages being turned.

Stress patterns in two-syllable words

Listen to the first extract of the sermon.

Jehovah's Witnesses believe that God created the world and the first human beings, Adam and Eve, lived in a state of paradise in the Garden of Eden. But

because they broke God's commandments, this paradise was 'lost'. The speaker
is describing what the world will be like when it returns to being a paradise after
the 'great tribulation', when God will rid the world of suffering and wickedness.

Sequence I

. . . can you just begin to imagine now the set-up that will return the – this earth to
a- a paradise can you even begin to imagine a paradise can you very difficult to
imagine a paradise isn't it it just imagine for example that when you leave the hall
this morning you go out of here and every individual that you meet loves you and
5   has your good at heart can you even begin to imagine what that will be that's part
of the paradise you see can you begin to imagine that uh for example you'll be able
to throw away your glasses throw away your walking sticks your backache will uh
gradually get better and do you know a saying that you won't be able to use any
more in conversation I don't know what will be- I don't know what we'll replace
10 it with hello how are you why won't we ever say hello how are you because the
answer is well what do you expect me to be like [he laughs and the congregation
laughs] I'm fit and healthy and perfect do you see so we'll get fed up with saying
hello how are you won't we and there are so many things that you can now begin
to conjure up your mind and that this global paradise will in fact be earth-wide
15 . . .

Exercise I

Using the transcript, find all the two syllable words and place a mark in front of
the syllable which has the accent, like this: be′gin.

Placement of stress in words is related to the following:

(a) the structure of the word – is it simple or is it complex? A complex word is
made up of identifiable parts – suffixes or prefixes plus a 'root' or 'base'.
For example, the word 'unthinkable' has a prefix (un), a root (think) and a
suffix (able). A complex word can also be composed of two parts that themselves can be separate words, such as 'make-up', 'homework', 'weeping
willow'.

(b) the grammatical category the word belongs to (noun, verb, adjective, etc.)

(c) the number of syllables in the word

(d) the composition of those syllables, e.g. is there a consonant following a diphthong ('recon<u>cile</u>') or a short vowel followed by two consonants ('amuse<u>ment</u>'), and so on?

Exercise 2

Divide these words into two groups: those that have the stress on the first syllable and those with the stress on the second.

Decide which vowels the speaker uses in the syllables which are stressed, and write in the appropriate symbol above the letter(s).

Verb patterns

As mentioned above, the stress pattern of an English word is related to the grammatical category to which it belongs and the structure of the syllables of that word in terms of its vowels and consonants. There seems to be a tendency for verbs in English to behave according to the following 'rules' (see PE5 10.3.1.):

(1) If a verb has a second syllable which ends with a long vowel or diphthong, or with either of these followed by single consonant, then that second syllable will be stressed.

(2) If a verb has a second syllable where there is a short vowel followed by two consonants, then that second syllable will be stressed.

Question 1

Examine your list of words with the pattern _'. Do you find any verbs which follow either of the two patterns above?

Noun patterns

There seems to be a tendency for nouns in English to behave according to the following 'rules':

(1) If the second syllable contains a short vowel, then the first syllable will be prominent.

(2) If the second syllable doesn't have a short vowel, then it (the second syllable) will be stressed.

Question 2

Examine your list of words with the pattern ′_. Do you find any nouns which follow these patterns?

Question 3

As well as nouns and verbs, prepositions, adjectives, and conjunctions seem to behave according to the same patterns.

Check these words: (1) 'because' (2) 'away' (3) 'even' (4) 'able', 'better', 'healthy', 'many', 'global', 'perfect'.

Question 4

Are there any words in your lists that do not fit into these patterns?

More practice of patterns in two-syllable words

Question 5

Listen to this extract. It is a continuation of Sequence 1. Make two lists as you did in Exercise 1, and check your lists for words that adhere to these tendencies and ones that are exceptions.

Sequence 2

. . . we'll prove that it'll be earth-wide look at Psalm 2 Psalm 2 [pages rustle and coughs] see verse 1 it says why have the nations been in tumult and the national groups themselves kept muttering an empty thing the kings of earth take their stand and high officials themselves have massed together as one against Jehovah and
5   against his anointed one saying let us tear their bands apart and cast their cords away from us see there is one thing that this world is united in that's the only thing that is that they don't want god's rulership it says in verse 4 the very ones sitting in the heavens will laugh Jehovah himself will hold them in derision at that time he will speak to them in his anger and in his hot displeasure he will disturb them
10 saying I even I have installed my king upon Zion my holy mountain . . .

let me refer to the decree of Jehovah he has said to me you are my son I today have become your father ask of me that I may give nations as your inheritance and the

ends of the earth as your own possession global paradise the ends of the earth as
your possession he said you will break them with an iron sceptre as though a
15   potter's vessel you will dash them to pieces

Patterns in words of three syllables or more

We'll use the next two extracts to look at words with three or more syllables.

In the first of these two extracts (Sequence 3) the speaker's theme is 'human beings were not created by God to rule themselves, but to be ruled by God'. Then, he outlines what qualities are required to 'rule the world'. (This is Sequence 4.) In both of these extracts there are several words with three or more syllables.

Exercise 3

Find all the words with three or more syllables in the two extracts and mark which syllable seems to be the most prominent in each word.

Sequence 3

. . . it does not belong to man to direct his step why not well look in Genesis one
twenty eight and see what God said to man when he first blessed him and gave him
his commission toward this earth Genesis one verse twenty eight it says and God
went on to say let us make man in our image according to our likeness and let them
5   have in subjection the fish of the sea the flying creatures of the heavens and the
domestic animals and all the earth and every moving animal that is moving upon
the earth so why is man not capable of directing his own steps or ruling himself
because he was created to rule the animals he was not created to rule himself the
Bible makes it very clear that during that period of time that Adam and Eve
10   enjoyed happiness and peace in paradise earth the Bible makes it very clear that in
the breezy part of the day God used to communicate with Adam and anything that
was necessary to tell him he used to tell him at that time and they enjoyed this very
happy relationship but man's rule came direct from the heavens direct from God
man was made created to be ruled by God he was not created to rule himself and
15   he certainly was not created to rule other men and that's why the uh u world is in
such a state today that man is trying to uh run on the wrong c- course he's the
wrong horse for the wrong course do you see . . .

Sequence 4

. . . and uh if we just think for a moment what would be required for somebody to rule this earth in righteousness perhaps we can see why it is that mankind can never ever fulfil that commission let me just highlight six things that would be required for somebody to rule this earth in righteousness first of all he would need
5 absolute authority absolute authority then he wouldn't be obliged to keep reconciling the conflicting opinions of many other people which is what rulership-leaders are up against today so he would need absolute authority can you think of any man that you know on this earth to whom you would want to give absolute authority can you think of any man who could handle absolute authority in addition to
10 absolute authority he would need a perfect law to follow a perfect law to follow not a law that's changed every time a new government comes in a perfect law to follow and in addition point number three he would need the wisdom and the love needed in order to follow that law towards everyone's benefit everyone's benefit can you think of any of the world leaders that so far fulfil those three requirements
15 the fourth one he would need a complete knowledge of every detail not only of human nature but of the ecology in which we live a complete knowledge of human nature and our ecology why because isn't it true to say that many of the most perplexing problems that face mankind today have to do with things like earth's food production with pollution so he would need a complete knowledge of human
20 nature and a complete knowledge of our ecology and number five he would also have to be concerned with every individual over whom he was ruling not people en masse but every individual he would have to be concerned for their personal welfare can you think of any leader that you know so far that fits those things and finally he would have to have the ability to know what is in the minds and the
25 hearts of every individual so that he can get to their hearts and get full cooperation from each one do you see this is a hopeless task for man . . .

Patterns in complex words

Several of the three + syllable words are 'complex' words – words with a 'root' or 'base' and one or more prefixes or suffixes.

Question 1

Find examples of words in the two extracts with the following suffixes: -ship, -ing, -ment, -ness, and -ly.

Notice that if we remove the suffix and 'reconstruct' the root, and then compare the stress pattern of the root by itself and the root in the complex word, we see that these suffixes do not change the shape of that root. For example, if the first syllable of the root is prominent, then in the form with the suffix that syllable is also prominent.

Here are some examples from Sequence 3:

'happy	'happiness	re'lation	re'lationship
di'rect	di'recting	'certain	'certainly

⚲ Question 2

Find more examples of words with these suffixes in Sequence 4, and examine the stress patterns of the roots as above.

Types of suffixes

Suffixes which have no effect on the accentual pattern of the root are called 'accent-neutral' suffixes. As we have seen from Question 1, they include the suffixes in English used in verbs, e.g. '-ing' as in 'directing', and to form adverbs – '-ly' as in 'certain'/'certainly'. The suffix '-y', used to make adjectives from nouns, is also an accent-neutral suffix ('syrup'/'syrupy'). (See PE5 10.3.2.)

Exercise 4

Examine Sequences 3 and 4 for words with the suffixes: -ion, -ty. What do you notice about the stress placement in the root, when you compare the root by itself as a word, and when it occurs in the complex word form?

Suffixes which change the accentual shape of a word when they are attached can be called 'accent-fixing suffixes' (PE5 10.3.2).

Placement of stress in compound words

In Sequences 1–4 there are several **compound** words. These are words which are composed of two or more roots, but they behave exactly like single words. In the spelling, the two roots can be separated by a hyphen ('dark-haired'), a space ('bus conductor'), or they can be written as one word ('daybreak'). (See PE5 10.3.5.)

Exercise 5

Mark the stress-pattern of these compound words:

Words from Sequence 1: set-up   walking stick   backache   earth-wide
Words from Sequence 4: mankind   highlight

Question 1

What range of patterns do you find?

The pronunciation of words with two or more weak/unaccented syllables

Secondary stress

When a word has more than one syllable before or after the prominent syllable, one of these less prominent syllables will 'gain' prominence. It receives what is called 'secondary stress'. This phenomenon seems to be based on a rhythmical tendency in English to alternate more prominent and less prominent syllables. (See PE5 10.3.4.)

Exercise 6

Listen to how the speaker pronounces the words 'reconciling' and 'cooperation' in Sequence 4. Which syllable is most prominent, and which is the *next* most prominent?

Deletion of syllables

In words where there is a sequence of unaccented syllables, speakers can be heard to delete one of the weak vowels, so that the number of syllables in the word is reduced by one. An example is 'comparable' ['kɒmpərəbəl] with four syllables which might be pronounced as ['kɒmprəbəl] or 'national' [naʃənəl] with three syllables, which might be pronounced with only two syllables [naʃnəl]. (See PE5 10.6.)

Exercise 7

Listen to the way the speaker pronounces the following words and transcribe his pronunciation. The number of syllables the words *could* have (in the most explicit and slow pronunciation) is given in brackets after each word.

From Sequence 2: national (3); muttering (3)
From Sequence 3: necessary (4)
From Sequence 4: government (3); individual (5) (occurs three times); finally (3)

Use of intonation

In Sequence 4 the speaker's purpose is to demonstrate how ill-suited human beings are as rulers of the earth. As he outlines the 'six things that would be required to rule this earth in righteousness' he emphasizes the enormity of the task through the use of repetition and by posing questions to his listeners.

Exercise 8

Below are the sections of his sermon where he uses repetition and questions to make his points. Listen to these sections, and try to draw a diagram of the intonation patterns he uses. The top and bottom lines of the stave represent the highest and lowest points in his use of pitch. Use level lines and curving lines to represent the rises and falls of his voice.

first of all he would need absolute authority absolute authority
then he wouldn't be obliged to keep reconciling the conflicting
opinions of many other people which is what rulership-leaders

are up against today so he would need absolute authority can you
think of any man that you know on this earth to whom you would

_____

_____

want to give absolute authority can you think of any man who

_____   _____

_____   _____

could handle absolute authority in addition to absolute authority

_____

_____

he would need a perfect law to follow a perfect law to follow not a law that's changed every time a new government's come in

_____

_____

a perfect law to follow and in addition point number three he would need the wisdom and love needed in order to follow that law

_____

_____

towards everyone's benefit everyone's benefit . . .

_____

_____

. . . the fourth one he would need a complete knowledge of every detail

_____

_____

not only of human nature but of the ecology in which we live a

_____

_____

complete knowledge of human nature and our ecology why . . .

_____

_____

so he would need a complete knowledge of human nature and a

_____

_____

complete knowledge of our ecology and number five he would also

_____

_____

have to be concerned with every individual over whom he was

_____

_____

ruling not people en masse but every individual . . .
and finally he would have to have the ability to know what is in

_____

_____

the minds and the hearts of every individual so that . . .

As well as the use of intonation and stress, pause is very important in the delivery of this part of the sermon. Some of the pauses are very long, and seem to function to focus the listeners' attention on particular points.

Exercise 9

Listen again to the excerpts in Exercise 8 and mark the pauses you hear with a '+' sign.

Now listen to this excerpt from the sermon which follows Sequence 4; pauses have been removed using a special software programme.

The process of vowel neutralization or vowel reduction

In Sequence 1 the word 'you' is used a total of 19 times. This is partly a product of his technique of addressing his audience directly, and encouraging them to speculate on the return of paradise. As part of this process he also uses short questions such as 'do you see', 'do you know' and poses several questions with the words 'can you imagine'.

The words 'you' and 'your' as well as the words 'can' and 'do' are examples of common English words – usually grammatical or function words – which have varying pronunciations. In the short exchange 'Who's going to wash the dishes?' '**You** are' the word would be pronounced as [juː], but 'you' can also be pronounced with a schwa [jə] or with a short vowel in the general area of [ʊ]. In a traditional marriage ceremony, when the bride and groom say 'I do', they will use the [uː] vowel; but in most other uses as an auxiliary verb, it will have [ə] or [ʊ].

In the case of 'can', a very emphatic statement such as 'yes I *can*' will be pronounced with [a], but very often speakers use a schwa [kən]. The form of such words when said in isolation or when emphasized is referred to as their 'strong' forms; the versions with a schwa or 'reduced' vowel are called **weak forms**.

Exercise 10

Question 1

Listen to Sequence 1 again. How many occurrences are there of the strong forms of 'you', 'can', and 'do'? How many occurrences are there of the weak forms?

Another word with both strong and weak forms is the preposition 'to'. In fact the strong form is very rarely used. It can occur when a speaker is making a contrast, as for example in 'I said, "Where are you going **to** not where are you coming **from**"'! The preposition 'to' has two weak forms, depending on whether a consonant or a vowel follows it:

(a) before a consonant it will be pronounced as [tə] as in 'When do you want to leave?' [təliːv]

(b) before a vowel at the beginning of the next word, it will be pronounced as [tʊ], as in 'When do you want to eat?' [tʊiːt]

Question 2

Listen to Sequence 1 again, and locate the occurrences of these two weak versions.

Pronunciation and speech style

One of the features of the style of this sermon is that the speaker shifts between very slow and deliberate speech, when he is reading aloud or setting out his argument in a very emphatic way (as in Sequence 4) and very colloquial speech, when he is addressing his audience and trying to bring them into his way of thinking using common everyday examples. An example of this very colloquial style is Sequence 5. He is trying to explain a phrase in Psalm 2 Verse 1 about Jesus: 'for his anger flares up easily'.

One characteristic of colloquial speech in English is that the speaker will use many weak syllables and consonant modifications and deletions. There will be groups of words/phrases that will be pronounced very quickly.

Sequence 5

. . . have you ever tried to light a fire with damp wood have you very difficult isn't it you keep blowing and puffing don't you you get a little ember and you keep on blowing what about when you light a fire with tinder-dry wood shwhoosh doesn't it that's what it means it means that when Jesus Christ does cleanse this earth of
5 wickedness and removes the wicked it won't take very long it won't take very long see there's no point in it taking long because no one's going to enjoy it Jehovah's not going to enjoy it Jesus is not going to enjoy it they don't want to kill anybody so it won't take long once the decision has been made it won't take long do you see but before it happens Jehovah says kiss the son that he may not become
10 incensed and you may not perish from the way . . .

Exercise 11

Below are transcriptions of some instances of rapid colloquial speech from Sequence 5. Listen to the whole extract and try to locate where these pronunciations occur.

(a) havjə

(b) ɪnəʔ

(c) jəˈgɛʔəlɪʔlˈɛmbə

(d) ɪʔˈwoʊnˈteɪkˈvɛriˈlɒŋ

(e) ˈnoʊwɒnzˈgənəɪnˈdʒɔɪʔ

(f) dəjəsiː

Looking back

In this unit we have focused on several areas. We have investigated word stress patterns in polysyllabic words, and seen that the position of stress seems to be related to rules having to do with syllable structure. However, the position of stress is not absolutely fixed – we need to take the phrase into account as well. We have worked on intonation patterns, and examined how length of pauses can be manipulated by a speaker for particular effects. We have seen that speakers pronounce words differently, changing their vowels and consonants, even deleting vowels and consonants, and that this is a normal part of spoken English.

Tasks for extension and discussion

Take any other sequence in this workbook and analyse the word stress patterns you find.

Using another part of the sermon, practise listening to intonation patterns, or look for a section where the speaker seems to be manipulating pauses for effect. Mark these pauses with a '+' and discuss what particular effects they might have on listeners.

One of the accent-attracting suffixes in English is '-ese', as in 'Japanese' or 'Chinese'. Assemble a group of objects (or pictures of objects) which are from countries that have this suffix in the adjective form (Portugal, the Lebanon, Japan, etc.). Ask a group of people to try to guess where they are from. As they are talking, try to note whether stress is placed on '-ese-, as in 'I think it's Japan'ese', or whether stress is shifted earlier in the adjective, as in 'That must be a 'Japanese fan'.

Unit 6 Key and comments

EXERCISE I AND 2

Pattern _'   Pattern '_

begin	morning	even
return	able	glasses
away	walking*	better
replace	saying	answer
because	healthy	perfect
hello	many	conjure
expect	global	

---

* 'set-up', 'backache' and 'earth-wide' are compound nouns and will be discussed in Exercise 5. The word 'walking' is part of what may also be considered to be a compound noun.

Question 1

'Replace' follows tendency 1 – it has a diphthong /eɪ/ followed by /s/.

If we look at 'return', for this speaker, who doesn't pronounce any 'r' in the spelling occurring after a vowel as /r/, but produces a long vowel instead /ɛː/, this also follows tendency 1. For speakers who pronounce 'r' after vowels and before a consonant, this word has the structure of two final consonants /-rn/ and therefore follows tendency 2.

'Expect' with a short vowel followed by two consonants in the second syllable also follows tendency 2.

Question 2

The words 'morning', 'glasses', 'saying' and 'answer' all have a short vowel in the second syllable and the stress is on the first syllable, following tendency 1 for nouns.

'Hello' has a diphthong (which counts as a long vowel) in the second syllable, and that syllable is stressed, following tendency 2.

Question 3

1 'because' has the long vowel /ɔː/ followed by one consonant /z/ (verb tendency 1).
2 'away' ends with a diphthong, so fits verb tendency 1.
3 'even' has a short vowel plus one consonant in syllable two, so it follows noun tendency 1.
4 The adjectives 'able', 'better' 'healthy', 'many', 'global' and 'perfect' all have short vowels in syllable two so fit in with noun tendency 1.

Question 4

'Begin' doesn't fit either of these two patterns for verbs, nor does 'conjure'.

Question 5

(Words in this extract which have already been discussed are not included below.)

Pattern _'	Pattern '_	
themselves	nations	tumult
against	empty	saying

Pattern _'	Pattern '_	
himself	very	sitting
disturb	heavens	anger
installed	Zion	holy
refer	mountain	father
decree	nations	iron
today	sceptre	potter
become	vessel	pieces

All the words in the lists fit the tendencies for nouns and verbs, and the three adjectives ('empty', 'holy' and 'iron') also conform. The verb 'become' is an exception; and the words with '-self' don't conform. All words with '-self' have stress on this second syllable. The first syllable can be stressed when making a contrast, e.g. 'He did it <u>him</u>self, without any help from you at all' (Kreidler 1997: 219).

EXERCISE 3 **Question 1 and Question 2**

Below are the 3+ syllable words in Sequence 3 (in order of occurrence). Note that the syllable divisions of the written forms below are those that dictionaries give; in other words, 'commission' is not pronounced [kəm'mɪʃən] with two bi-labial nasals!)

'Genesis   ac'cording   com'mission   sub'jection
do'mestic   'animals   'capable   di'recting   cre'ated
'happiness
'paradise   com'municate   'necessary   re'lationship
'certainly

Here are the words in Sequence 4. (Words that occur in Sequence 3 are not repeated.)

re'quired   'somebody   'righteousness   abso'lute   au'thority
recon'ciling   con'flicting   op'inions   'rulership
'government   ad'dition   'everyone   'benefit   re'quirements
e'cology   per'plexing   pro'duction   pol'lution
indi'vidual   'personal   'finally   a'bility   cooper'ation

Note that the word 'every' is no longer pronounced with three syllables as the spelling would seem to indicate it once was. Like 'evening' the vowel after the first consonant has long since been deleted. (See PE5 10.6.)

These words always have stress on the syllable **before** the suffix. If we compare the stress pattern of 'final' and 'finality', we see that the first syllable is stressed in the root – 'final, but the second syllable is stressed when the suffix is added – fi'nality. So the suffix can bring about a change in stress placement. Of course, in the word 'pollute', the stress is already on the second syllable, so when '-ion' is added, the position of stress doesn't change.

(See PE5 10.3.5 for a full discussion.)

In compounds, primary stress is often on the first element ('**set-up**, '**walking-stick**, '**backache**, '**highlight**) but we have **man'kind** as a counter example. However, compare the pattern of **man'kind** with '**man-eater** and '**man-hunt**. When the speaker first says **earth-wide**, he seems to put equal stress on both elements. However, the second time he says it, the accent falls on '-wide'.

This word is a good example of how the accent can shift in a word. The speaker uses it both times at the end of a phrase; if he had used it *within* a phrase in a position before a strong syllable, the stress would probably be on 'earth'. So he might have said '**earth-wide** '**paradise**. Compare **world-'wide** with '**world-wide** '**web**. Here are some more examples:

Accent on part two	Accent shift to part one
It's brand-'new.	a 'brand-new 'coat
She's so old-'fashioned.	an 'old-fashioned 'dress
Your hands are ice-'cold.	I need an 'ice-cold 'drink.

The stress pattern of compounds words can vary according to the variety of English. For example, in American English you'll hear **peanut-'butter,** but in British English you'll hear '**peanut-butter.**

These words seem to have secondary stress (marked with *): *recon'ciling co*oper'ation.

(The number of syllables appears in brackets.)

Sequence 2: 'muttering' seems to have three syllables, but in 'national' he moves from /ʃ/ to /n/ and deletes the vowel represented by the letter 'o', making it have two syllables.

Sequence 3: 'necessary' has four syllables.

Sequence 4: 'government' has three. The first time the speaker says 'individual' it has five syllables; the second and third times he says it, it has four (/ɪndɪvɪdʒʊl/). The word 'finally' is pronounced with three syllables.

Pronunciations without deletion seem to predominate; this is probably linked to the formality of the speech situation and the speaker's deliberate, slow, preaching style.

EXERCISE 8 AND 9

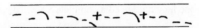

first of all he would need absolute authority absolute authority then he wouldn't be obliged to keep reconciling the conflicting opinions of many other people which is what rulership- leaders

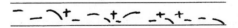

are up against today so he would need absolute authority can you think of any man that you know on this earth to whom you would

want to give absolute authority can you think of any man who

could handle absolute authority in addition to absolute authority

he would need a perfect law to follow a perfect law to follow not a law that's changed every time a new government's come in a perfect law to follow and in addition point number three he would need the wisdom and love needed in order to follow that law

towards everyone's benefit everyone's benefit . . .

. . . the fourth one he would need a complete knowledge of every detail

not only of human nature but of the ecology in which we live a

complete knowledge of human nature and our ecology why . . .

so he would need a complete knowledge of human nature and a

complete knowledge of our ecology and number five he would also

have to be concerned with every individual over whom he was

ruling not people en masse but every individual . . . and finally he would have to have the ability to know what is in the minds and the hearts of every individual so that . . .

This extract illustrates very well how intonation is exploited by speakers to show points of focus, emphasis and contrast, and to signal non-finality. Notice the rising tones used as the speaker progresses through his list of six things. Note also that when words are repeated, such as 'authority', 'law', 'individual', etc., they are pronounced low in the pitch range, or have a fall-rise pattern. This fall-rise pattern here has been identified as a tone used for 'referring' to something which is already part of the context of the talk. (See Brazil (1994) and Bradford (1988).)

EXERCISE 10 **Question 1**

There are 17 occurrences of 'you' in the extract. The strong form is used in 'hello how are you' (three times), most probably because of its final position in the utterances. Strong forms are used in 'every individual that you meet loves you and has your good at heart' (lines 4–5). The last occurrence towards the end of the extract, 'so many things that you can now begin', also seems to have [u:].

This speaker is among those English speakers whose pronunciation of 'you' can vary depending on whether a vowel or a consonant follows in the next word. Before a consonant, he uses [jə] as his weak form, as in 'this morning you go out' (line 4). Before a vowel, he uses a vowel in the area of [ʊ] as in 'can you **e**ven'(line 2). In the short phrases 'you see' (line 6), 'do you know' (line 8), 'do you see' (line 12) the vowel in 'you' is clearly a schwa.

Some speakers do not follow this pattern and will use [jə] exclusively as their weak form, before consonants **and** vowels.

There are some occurrences of the strong form of 'can' with /a/ here because of the focus he is putting on 'can you . . .' to convey the difficulty of imagining paradise. The first five uses of this phrase have the /a/ vowel. He uses the form with schwa at the end of the excerpt when he says 'and you can now begin . . .'

There are no occurrences of the strong form of 'do'. When he says the phrase 'do you see' (line 12), there is no vowel at all [djəsi:]. When he says 'do you know' (line 18) there is also no vowel, and the [d] has merged with the [j] to produce [dʒ] [dʒənoʊ]. This also happens in the little conversation where he says 'what do you expect . . . I'm fit' (line 11–12) [wʊdʒə]. In 'you see' at line 6 we could say that the word 'do' is as weak as a word can get – it has been deleted completely!

EXERCISE 10 Question 2

/tʊ/ occurs in: to imagine (line 1) to a paradise (line 2).
/tə/ occurs in: throw away (line 7) to use anymore (line 8) to be like (line 11)
to conjure up (line 14).

EXERCISE 11

In the transcript below the phrases are underlined and marked with the appropriate letter.

> . . . have you ever tried to light a fire with damp wood a) <u>have you</u> very difficult b)
> <u>isn't it</u> you keep blowing and puffing don't you c) <u>you get a little ember</u> and you
> keep on blowing what about when you light a fire with tinder-dry wood shwhoosh
> doesn't it that's what it means it means that when Jesus Christ does cleanse this
> earth of wickedness and removes the wicked d) <u>it won't take very long</u> it won't
> take very long see there's no point in it taking long because e) <u>no one's going to</u>
> <u>enjoy it</u> Jehovah's not going to enjoy it Jesus is not going to enjoy it they don't
> want to kill anybody so it won't take long once the decision has been made it won't
> take long f) <u>do you see</u> but before it happens Jehovah says kiss the son that he may
> not become incensed and you may not perish from the way . . .

In some of these phrases we see the use of the **glottal stop** symbolized by [ʔ].
This sound is made by bringing the two vocal cords together and then releasing
them quickly to produce a plosive sound. In the speaker's accent this sound is
often used as a variant of /t/.

Note that we also have in this extract an occurrence of the strong form of
'does' in 'when he does cleanse' at line 4. Also, the two other phrases with
'going to' contrast with e) because the pronunciation is [goʊɪŋtʊ].

'women was strong in them days'

Preview

These extracts are taken from an interview between a man and a woman about village life in Cornwall in the early part of the twentieth century. We will be focusing on the woman's speech, and examining her use of phrasing and intonation. We will also analyse some of her vowel and consonant pronunciations.

Background

When this recording was made, the woman was in her seventies. She was living in a cottage in Pendeen, a small village in Cornwall. She had lived in this part of Cornwall all her life. Another local, a man in his fifties, was asking her questions about her family, about everyday life in Cornwall at that time, and about the tin-mining industry. For 3000 years tin-mining was the most important industry in Cornwall. It continued into the twentieth century but declined until the 1980s, when the last few mines were closed. They are talking in the sitting room of her cottage. At one point in the recording you can hear the mantelpiece clock chiming.

Listen to all the sequences to get an overview of the conversation.

Exercise 1

At the beginning of Sequence 1, they have been talking about her great-grandfather, who was a 'tin-dresser'. (In the tin mining industry, a tin-dresser prepared the tin ore for smelting by cleaning it and removing the non-metallic substances.)

Question 1

Listen to the sequence. When you hear a pause in the woman's speech, mark it with a vertical line on the transcript.

In the transcript 'M' stands for the man, and 'W' for the woman.

M: and where – do you remember where your father – great-grandfather where they all lived did you ever know

W: yes my great-grandfather lived over Flintshire (?) which is the other side of Geevor mine over between Geevor and Levant there's a little cottage over there and
5 he used to live there and he lived there for a good many years I think he had most of his family there and then they went up to Trewellard and that was when our family went in to live with him (M: oh yeah) yes 'cause his wife died and uh we went in with him that's right

Dividing speech into phrases according to where the speaker pauses

If we divide her speech into units based on her pauses, we see that some of these units bounded by pause correspond to single words (Flintshire/Trewellard/yes), and others correspond to groups of words or phrases. If we look at the syntactic structure of the groups of words, we see that some are noun phrases (our family); some are prepositional phrases (of Geevor mine), some are clauses with both a subject and a verbal element (we went in with him), and some seem to be 'unfinished', for example, 'and that was when' and 'which is the other side'. Here is a complete list of the pause-bounded units in this extract:

Single words: Flintshire   Trewallard   yes   over   yes
Groups of words:
of Geevor mine
between Levant and Geevor there's a little cottage over there
and he used to live there
and he lived there for a good many years I think he had most of his family there

we went in with him
that's right
my great-grandfather lived over
which is the other side
and then they went up to
and that was when
our family
went in to live with him
'cause his wide died and uh

The total number of units is 18.

Changes in the pitch of the voice within phrases

As we have seen, when we speak, the vibrations that take place in the larynx produce a pitch or tone. Speakers can do two things with the pitch of their voices: they can hold a particular pitch on a syllable or word or they can vary the pitch during the syllable, making it move higher or drop lower.

Question 2

Listen to the last word or syllable of the following phrases. How would you describe the tone or pitch of the last syllable?

over
my great-grandfather lived over
which is the other side
and then we went up to
and that was when
our family

Question 3

Now listen to the other groups again and underline the words or syllables where you hear the tone of her voice changing.

Flintshire
of Geevor mine
between Geevor and Levant   there's a little cottage there

and he used to live there for a good many years I think he had most of his children there
went into live with him
we went in with him
that's right

By listening to the speaker's use of pause and moving pitch, we can divide any stretch of speech into phrases. Just as a written text can be divided into sentences or paragraphs, a spoken text can be divided into phrases. These phrases are called 'tone units', and they are useful in the analysis of the intonation of spoken English.

If we look again at those points where the woman chooses to pause, it seems clear that some of these pauses are 'hesitation pauses' – she is thinking of what to say or trying to remember names of places, the order of events, etc. These are also identifiable by her use of 'uh' or 'um', as for example in ''cause his wife died and uh . . .' In other cases we could say that she is dividing her talk into *chunks of information* for the listener and is using pause as a signal of the boundaries of these information chunks.

Where are the boundaries of tone units?

Notice that there are two quite long stretches of speech where the woman doesn't pause:

> between Geevor and Levant there's a little cottage there

> and he lived there for a good many years I think he had most of his family there

Although there is no audible pause within these stretches, we could divide each into two units on the basis that each has a word or syllable spoken with pitch movement. These are:

Levant   cottage   years   family

This would give us four units instead of two (or a total of 20 instead of 18) with each unit having a word which is made prominent for the listener by the use of moving pitch.

But if we are going to have units based on pitch movement somewhere *inside* the phrase, and not on the pauses at the edges, how do we decide where these tone units begin and end? There are a few possible ways of doing this.

Sometimes a change of tempo or rhythm can be perceived at the boundary of a tone unit. Listen to how quickly the woman says the words 'there's a little . . .' Because of this sudden spurt of speed which she seems to use to set this group of words apart from the previous group, we can place a tone unit boundary after the word 'Levant'.

Another criterion is based on the observation that speakers often start a tone unit on the same pitch. We could call this a 'home-pitch' – each time a speaker starts a new tone unit they 'return to home' or 'go back to start'. Using this criterion we can put a tone unit boundary after the word 'years' because on the next word 'I' she seems to return to her 'home pitch'.

Below is Sequence 1 with tone units of the woman marked.

M: and where   do you remember where your father   great-grandfather where they all lived   did you ever know

W: | yes | my great-grandfather lived over | Flintshire | which is the other side | of Geevor mine | over | between Geevor and Levant | there's a little cottage over there | and he used to live there | and he lived there for a good many years | I think he had most of his family there | and then they went up to | Trewellard | and that was when | our family | went in to live with him | (M: oh yeah) | yes | 'cause his wife died and uh | we went in with him | that's right |

Difficulty of tone unit identification

Identifying tone units is sometimes very difficult. Phoneticians will disagree about where to put boundaries when listening to the same recording. Slightly different criteria have been proposed and different analysts use slightly different systems. Sometimes we can even say that a speaker produces an 'incomplete tone unit' because there is no moving pitch even though there might be pauses. This can happen because the speaker has been interrupted, or has 'self-interrupted' because they have changed their minds about what to say. The most important point to remember is that dividing a spoken text into tone units helps us to examine how speakers convey meaning to their listeners.

Conveying meaning through the intonation of the voice

As an example of this, let's look at the way the woman says almost exactly the same sequence of words in two separate tone units:

line 7 (our family) went in to live with him
lines 7–8 we went in with him

    Notice that in the first occurrence, there is moving pitch on the word 'with', while in the second there is more moving pitch on 'him'. If we look only at the words the woman says, it might seem that she is simply repeating herself. But if we listen to the two tone units, there is a difference in the meaning she is conveying. In the first there is more focus on the fact that the family was now living all together. In the second tone unit there seems to be more of a contrast established between 'living with him' and 'living in our own house'.

Exercise 2

In Sequence 2 the woman has been asked about her grandfather. Listen for pauses, and mark them in some way. Then underline the words that seem to have the most prominent pitch movement. Then try to divide the sequence into tone units.

Sequence 2

M: and your grandfather you remember him W: yeah (M: better) no I didn't remember my grandfather (M: oh you didn't) no 'cause he died when I was young but my great-grandfather lived on see all that time because I think I must have been uh when my great-grandfather died I think I was about um thirteen fourteen some-
5   thing like that (M: hmm) he was eighty-six when he died

Intonation choice and information structure

In this sequence there are three tone units which contain the word 'died'. Listen to these tone units and mark the direction of pitch change you hear on this word.

a	b	c
'cause he died	when my great-grandfather died	when he died

    The first time the woman uses the word 'died' she uses a lot of pitch movement on it, first falling and then slightly rising. On the second and third occasions, the pitch of her voice is moving, but in a different way. In both cases the overall pitch is low, and slightly rising.

What meanings do these different pitch movements convey? We could say that the first use of 'died' introduces the point of information about her grandfather's death to her listener. This fact explains why she doesn't remember him. There could have been several possible reasons for her not remembering him – her parents lived too far way for frequent visits, or her grandfather emigrated when she was still a baby, and so on.

Once the topic of 'dying' has been raised, it becomes part of the context or background to whatever she says next. What she does say next **adds** to this topic – she says how old she was when her great-grandfather died and how old he was when he died. So we could say that on the first occasion (tone unit a) she is telling her listener something new, whereas on the next two occurrences (tone units b and c) she is referring to a topic that has already been mentioned.

For any listener it is important to know what we are being *told* and what it is assumed we *know* or are already aware of. So speakers use different pitch movements in their speech to signal these basic distinctions. The contrast between information which is presented to the listener as 'new', and information that is 'old' or already raised is very important in conversational English.

When he was a boy . . .

Here is another example of a chunk of information presented as 'new' to the listener and then subsequently referred to later in the conversation. The phrases that we will be discussing are in bold.

In this Sequence the woman is talking about the men in her family who worked in the tin mines. She says that her great-grandfather worked as a tin dresser, then her grandfather, and then her father followed in the family tradition, starting in the mines 'as a boy'.

Sequence 3

W: yes he was a tin dresser down Levant mine well as you can see from the paper he was down there for sixty some odd years a tin dresser and then my grandfather took over and after that my father well he worked there **as a boy** and uh well they spent most of their lives down Levant

[Based on his own knowledge of the mining industry, the man then made a remark about her great-grandfather.]

> M: so he was there when the mine was working at its height
>
> W: must have been (M: busiest really) that's right yes my father was there **when he was a boy** I got his photo somewhere **when he was a boy** down there

Notice that although she has already told her listener that her father worked in the mines as a boy, he hasn't made any comment about that fact, and perhaps she chooses to repeat this point of information.

In this part of their conversation, the woman says the words 'when he was a boy' twice. The first time she seems to 'tell' her listener 'he was a boy when he worked in the mines' by the use of falling pitch movement. On the second occurrence, the new point of information is the photo she has: 'was a boy', which is now part of the context, is said on low pitch rising slightly.

Exercise 3

In the next excerpt, the woman has been asked about women's lives in Cornwall during the early part of the century. Listen to the pitch of her voice on the words/syllables which are underlined in the transcript. Note whether you hear a falling tone or a rising tone.

Sequence 4

> M: and what about the women how were they affected how did they eh what sort of
> social life did they have W: never had much social life at <u>all</u> they was <u>home</u> work-
> ing in the <u>house</u> and of course there use to be a lot of them who used to work <u>down</u>
> the mines you know on top used to call them the <u>bell maidens</u> and um of course
> 5 that's going back further I can't remember <u>that</u> but I've heard them <u>say</u> that you
> know that they used to wear <u>toussers</u> (?) and <u>bonnets</u> and they used to work down
> there 'cause women was <u>strong</u> in them <u>days</u> you know because I've heard my
> husband's mother <u>say</u> that her mother-in-law had twenty-two <u>children</u> and she used
> to make me laugh because she used to say they's like a <u>tea trade</u> comical really you
> 10 know like a <u>tea trade</u> twenty-two <u>children</u> M: where did they all live W: all here in
> the village scattered around like M: twenty-two children that's twenty-four people
> in the house W: I know but they used to sleep two and three and four in the bed
> and boys and girls together they never used to take no notice of that no and one
> look after the other I think the mother used to be baking and doin- cooking food
> 15 all the time and girls would do the work and so forth it was [laughs] I suppo- just
> took it for granted I suppose

❧ Question 1

Which type of pitch movement predominates in the first part of the sequence, up to the man's question? How would you account for this predominance in the woman's choice of pitch movement on these underlined items?

❧ Question 2

In the last part of this extract, the woman uses three phrases to express her own reaction to life in this ultra-large family: 'I know' (line 12), 'no' (line 13 (second occurrence)) and 'I suppose' (line 16). Listen to the pitch movement of these three phrases. How would you describe the pattern she uses? What meanings might this pattern convey to the listener?

Pitch range

In the course of this extract, the phrase 'twenty-two children' occurs three times. Listen to the two instances said by the woman and the third, said by the man. Notice that the overall pitch of the woman's voice is higher on the second occasion. It seems that to express her astonishment at the number of children, she carries out a 'step up' in pitch. We might draw a comparison between this 'intonation act' and the action of holding up an object of interest for someone else to see more clearly. Or, one could say that the intonation she uses on the second occasion expresses the same meaning as if she had said 'Can you imagine that?!'

In contrast to this behaviour, when the man says the phrase, his overall pitch is quite low. Perhaps we could gloss his meaning as 'I've taken in that information and I am considering what it really means.' He (or indeed another speaker) might have chosen to shift up in pitch to show his astonishment. Another intonational choice would have been a high rising pitch movement, that is, a rising tone which ends at the very top of a speaker's speaking voice.

When speakers exploit their ability to change the overall pitch of their voices – to switch between being a soprano, alto or baritone or bass, we say that they are using their *pitch range*. Roach (1991: 116) gives this definition:

> Each speaker has his or her own normal pitch range: a top level which is the highest pitch normally used by the speaker, and a bottom level that the speaker's voice normally does not go below. In ordinary speech, the intonation tends to take place within the lower part of the speaker's range, but in situations where strong feelings are to be expressed it is usual to make use of extra pitch height.

/h/ at the beginning of words

The pronunciation of /h/ in different accents of English varies a great deal. Below are transcriptions of phrases taken from Sequence 4. These transcriptions assume that orthographic 'h' will be pronounced as a period of voicelessness preceding the vowel. Listen to Sequence 4 again. If you hear her pronouncing an /h/ sound leave the transcription as it stands; if you hear no /h/, rewrite the relevant parts of the transcription to show this, or draw a cross through the /h/ symbol.

Question 1

nɛvər had mʌtʃ
never had much social life at all

ðeɪ wɒz hoʊm ... ɪn ði haʊs
they was home working in the house

bʌt aɪv hərd ...
but I've heard them say

... aɪv hərd maɪ hʌzbənz ...
because I've heard my husband's mother say

... hər mʌðərɪnlɔː had ...
that her mother-in-law had twenty-two children

Question 2

In the following extract (Sequence 5) the woman is talking about how she used to wash the clothes in the days before automatic washing machines. Words which are spelled with initial 'h' are underlined. Make a transcription of her pronunciation of these words.

<u>had</u> to carry the water from the well in buckets well I <u>have</u> since I been <u>here</u> because we never <u>had</u> water <u>here</u> when we came <u>here</u> (M: you didn't) no used to

go to that end short (?) out there where that square iron is stowed (?) and dip up buckets of water from there I carried so much as twelve buckets of a day when I been washing clothes I'd take one off and I'd feel my shoulders are achy I said that's carrying the water . . .

Question 3

How consistent is the woman's pronunciation of words spelled with 'h'? Listen again to Sequences 1 and 2. Since she is talking about male members of her family there are several occurrences of the pronouns 'he', 'his' and 'him' in these extracts – how does she pronounce these words?

Exercise 5

The pronunciation of words with 'r' in the spelling

In some varieties of English an /r/ is pronounced in all words with 'r' in the spelling. These are called **rhotic accents**. In other accents, in particular Received Pronunciation or '**RP**', which is the non-regional accent of the United Kingdom, speakers do not pronounce the 'r' after a vowel at the end of a word, or before a consonant, as in 'turn' or 'door'. These accents are termed non-rhotic. Listen to Sequence 4 again. There are several words where 'r' occurs in final position in the orthographic form of the word (e.g. 'never', 'further', 'remember', 'wear', etc.) or where 'r' occurs in the middle of a word before a consonant sound (e.g. 'working', of course', 'further', 'heard', etc.).

Does this Cornish woman have a 'rhotic' or a 'non-rhotic accent'?

Exercise 6

The pronunciation of words beginning with 'tr-'

In this next excerpt (Sequence 6) the man has asked the woman 'what did you have to heat the water up in?'(for washing clothes). Listen to her reply, and notice how she says the word 'tray' (used three times).

Sequence 6

. . . M: what did you have to heat the water up in W: a boiler on a slab iron boiler and down in that little room there that little dining room I had a sl- great slab in

there Cornish range you know (M: hm hm) and I used to put the boiler iron boiler
on that and boil them (M: you never had the detergent that you have these days did
5 they) used to have a tray a wood tray a long tray like and used to do and I had a
board that used to rub the clothes on they that was very dirty you know [laughs]
and then uh used to have another bath with bluing in 'im and a pan with starch in
'im [laughs] oohhh we were up here and there was no electric here when I come
here we had lamps to start out with yes we was here a good many years before we
10 had electric put in

The woman's pronunciation of the word 'tray' is a good example of **affrication**. An affricate is defined as '. . . any plosive whose release stage is performed
in such a way that considerable friction occurs approximately at the point where
the plosive stop is made . . .' (PE5 p. 57). In Unit 1, we looked at the sounds at
the beginning and end of '<u>ch</u>ur<u>ch</u> and '<u>j</u>u<u>dge</u>'. These are the palato-alveolar
affricates in the English consonant system, transcribed as /tʃ/ and /dʒ/.

In saying 'tray' the speaker is not producing a plosive [t], followed by the [r]
as she would in the word 'foo<u>tr</u>est'. The sound she produces is quite different.
First of all, the [t] is retracted (produced further back than usual) so it is post-
alveolar instead of alveolar. Second, the [r] is not a liquid, but a fricative. Third,
the [r] is devoiced – it matches the voicelessness of the [t]. We can use IPA
diacritics to represent these features: [t̠ɹ̥eɪ].

In English, words beginning with 'dr-', such as 'dress', 'draw', or 'drive' are
also pronounced with affrication, but because the [d] is voiced, the [r] will not
be devoiced.

These two sounds are very similar to the sounds /tʃ/ and /dʒ/, but there are
differences. As we have seen above, the place of articulation is post-alveolar, not
palato-alveolar. Also the period of friction for [tr-] and [dr-] is shorter than it is
for [tʃ] and [dʒ]. Say the following pairs of words and make sure you can hear
the difference:

| chap | trap | chew | true | truck | chuck | trunk | chunk |
| drug | jug | drain | Jane | dram | jam | drone | Joan |

Now here are some words with a sequence of [-tr-] or [-dr-] where there is no
affrication. Listen to the differences in pronunciation in the words where there is
affrication:

| breadroll vs. droll | handrake vs. drake |
| footramp vs. tramp | footrail vs. trail |

If you listen again to Sequence 4, you will hear another good example of affrication when the woman says 'they's like a tea <u>tr</u>ade'.

Plosives pronounced with affrication

Listen again to Sequence 5.

In this sequence there are two words with medial plosives: 'water' has a voiceless alveolar plosive [t] between the two vowels, and 'buckets' has a voiceless velar plosive [k] between the two vowels. If the closure made for these plosives is not released rapidly, then there will be a brief period of voiceless friction at the same place of articulation as the plosive. Plosives with this slow fricative release are said to be 'affricated'. In the word 'water' the plosive is voiceless and alveolar, so there might be a short voiceless alveolar [s] here; likewise in 'buckets' there might be a short voiceless velar [x].

We can use a superscript [s] or [x] to show the affrication:

[wɔːt^{s}ər]   [bʌk^{x}əts]

Exercise 7

In Sequence 5 the woman says the words 'water' and 'buckets' three times each. Listen to each occurrence, and mark whether you hear her using affrication or not:

had to carry the (1) water from the well in (1) buckets . . .
because we never had (2) water here . . .
dip up (2) buckets of (3) water from there . . .
twelve (3) buckets of a day . . .

Exercise 8

Make a transcription of the following phrases from Sequence 6.

(a) a boiler on a slab iron boiler
(b) and I used to put the boiler iron boiler on that and boil them
(c) and used to do
(d) and then uh used to have another bath with bluing in him and a pan with starch in him

(e) and there was no electric here when I come here
(f) we was here a good many years before we had electric put in

Looking back

In this unit we have worked on the notion of the tone unit, and extended our consideration of the meanings and uses of intonation. We have examined some specific features that make up this Cornish woman's accent – features which occur in many other varieties of English.

Tasks for consolidation or discussion

Get someone to tell you about episodes in their past, perhaps using family photographs. Make a recording, and analyse their use of intonation patterns.

Choose any of the sequences and analyse the speech into tone units, noting pauses, pitch changes, and so on. Are there any boundaries that you find particularly difficult to decide on?

Unit 7 Key and comments

EXERCISE I   Question 2

The words 'side', 'to', 'when', and the final syllables of 'over' (both occurrences) and 'family' and the hesitation sound 'uh' are all said on a mid tone, rather than high or low. Imagine someone counting from one to three. They might begin on a high pitch, and then move to 'two' on a mid pitch, with the tone of 'three' dropping low. The woman 'holds' this mid pitch – her voice does not glide higher or lower, so we might call it a 'steady' tone or a 'level' tone.

EXERCISE I   Question 3

In saying these words or syllables, the pitch of the woman's voice is changing or gliding, rather than being held steady on one pitch. There are two basic possibilities: (1) the pitch can go higher, or 'rise', or (2) the pitch can go lower or 'fall'. Speakers can also combine these two types of movement, and change the direction of pitch movement – first falling then rising or first rising and then falling.

EXERCISE 2

. . . | <u>no</u> | I didn't remember my grand<u>fa</u>ther | (you didn't) |<u>no</u>| 'cause he <u>died</u>| when I was <u>young</u>| but my great-grandfather lived <u>on</u>| see all that <u>time</u>| because I think I must have <u>been</u> uh| when my great-grandfather <u>died</u>| I think I was <u>about</u> um| thirteen four<u>teen</u>| something like <u>that</u>| (hmm)| he was eighty-<u>six</u>| when he <u>died</u>|

EXERCISE 3 **Question 1**

There is a high frequency of falling tones on the underlined words. The woman is giving information to the questioner. She assumes that he is unfamiliar with the 'bell maidens' and with women's lives in those times or he wouldn't have asked her. So we could say she is using these falling tones for 'telling'.

EXERCISE 3 **Question 2**

She uses quite a complex pitch movement: falling–rising–falling. It could be represented by this type of arrow ⌣⌢. When she uses this pitch movement on 'I know', it seems to convey that having 22 children and therefore 24 people living in one house is not a usual situation, but one worthy of comment. In using it on the word 'no', she seems to be doing the same thing – the fact that the sisters and brothers in a very large family would not have separate bedrooms or even beds to sleep in is seen to be unusual. The word 'no' itself is a repetition of 'never took no notice of that' i.e. 'no, they didn't'. Repetition can be another way speakers emphasize a point or call attention to the unusual or the unexpected.

In using this complex pitch movement on 'I suppose' she does not seem to be drawing attention to the unusual, but showing an attitude of uncertainty towards the statement she has just made – 'they took this way of living for granted'. We might paraphrase her meaning as: 'I think they must have taken this situation for granted, but maybe they *didn't* – maybe they were very aware of how different their lives were.

This discussion illustrates a crucial point about intonation. There seem to be tones that are strongly associated with particular general meanings or functions, for example signalling new information or background (contextually established information). But there are also pitch movements which seem to have different meanings in different contexts, in other words, they have 'local meanings'. Our example of this is the fall–rise–fall. This state of affairs shouldn't surprise us really, since words in a language behave in the same way. The word 'white' in the phrase 'white coffee' means something quite different from the word 'white' in 'white lie' or in 'white hot'.

EXERCISE 4   Question 1

nɛvəradmʌtʃ ...
never had much social life at all
ðeɪwɒzoʊm   ...   ɪnðiaʊs
they was home working in the house
    aɪvərd
but I've heard them say
        aɪvərdmaɪʔʌzbənz ...
because I've heard my husband's mother say
    ərmʌðərɪnlɔːad ...
that her mother-in-law had twenty-two children

Note that when she says 'husband's', she uses a glottal stop.

EXERCISE 4   Question 2

had
had to carry the water
    av
well I have
        ir
since I been here
        ad   iːr
we never had water here
            ir
when we came here

EXERCISE 4   Question 3

SEQUENCE 1
    i
and he used to live there
    i
and he lived there
        i ad   ɪz
I think he had most of his family there

ɪm
went into live with him

ɪm
we went in with him

SEQUENCE 2

i
'cause he died

hi i
he was 86 when he died

Based on this data, the woman seems to pronounce all the forms of the masculine pronouns (he/him/his) and the feminine pronoun 'her' without an [h] most of the time. She doesn't have an [h] in the nouns and verbs in the extracts (home/house/heard/husband) either. Of the three occasions she says 'here', none has [h]. There are four occurrences of 'had/have'. In 'had to carry the water' there is clearly an initial [h]. Note that she doesn't use the word 'I' or 'we' in this utterance, so perhaps [h] is pronounced in 'had' because this word is carrying the accent or stress.

EXERCISE 5

The woman has a rhotic accent.

EXERCISE 7

Affrication of 'water' and 'buckets' is as follows:

had to carry the (1) water {no} from the well in (1) buckets {yes}
because we never had (2) water {yes} here
dip up (2) buckets {no} of (3) water {no} from there
twelve (3) buckets {no} of a day

EXERCISE 8

ə bɔɪlərɒnəslaːbaɪərnbɔɪlər
(a) a boiler on a slab iron boiler

ənə justəpʊʔðəbɔɪləraɪərnbɔɪlərɒnðaʔənbɔɪlðəm
(b) and I used to put the boiler iron boiler on that and boil them

ənjuːstəduː

(c) and used to do

ənðɛn ʌ justə av ənʌðərbaːθwɪbluɪnɪnəm ənə paːnwɪθstartʃɪnəm

(d) and then uh used to have another bath with bluing in him and a pan with starch in him

ənðɛr wəznoʊələktrɪkiːrwɛn aɪkʌmiːr

(e) and there was no electric here when I come here

wiwəziːrəgʊdmɛnijɪrzbəfɔrwiadlɛktrɪkpʊtɪn

(f) we was here a good many years before we had electric put in

Some selected comments

In the nouns 'slab', 'bath' and 'pan' we can hear good examples of the woman's low front vowel /a/ which is here long – /aː/.

There are three nice examples of the pronunciation of the phrase 'used to' (in (b), (c) and (d)) with the connected speech modifications which are typical of English speakers: the /d/ has lost its voicing because of the following [t] and the vowel in 'to' is a schwa.

Note the use of an alveolar nasal as opposed to a velar nasal in 'bluing'.

Because both 'pan' and 'bath' are singular nouns, we must assume that when she says [əm] when referring to these containers, this corresponds to the pronoun 'him'. Many speakers of English would use the pronoun 'it' here, so it would seem that in this woman's dialect, pans and baths are masculine!

In (f) notice the simplifications of 'we was here' – 'was' has its weak form with schwa. In pronouncing the word 'electric', the woman deletes the initial vowel on the second occurrence.

'in Ghana'

Preview

We will be looking at a selection of features of pronunciation including speech rhythm, stress and intonation patterns, and vowel and consonant production.

Background

The extracts have been taken from a conversation between a university student in her final year and one of her tutors. We will be focusing on the student's pronunciation only. She is a woman in her late twenties, who was living in London at the time of recording. She was born in Ghana, and is multilingual. She speaks two varieties of the Akan Language, she learned English as a child through her schooling in Ghana (where it was the medium of instruction), and started learning French in school at the age of 12. After finishing her university degree, she plans to be a teacher of French.

Listen to all the sequences to get an overview of the conversation.

Sequence I

In this part of the conversation the speaker is explaining the festival of 'harvest'.

> harvest is just like um + every year they think you have to bring your + offering to
> God + so you have to set aside a special amount + so we have to really promote it
> + because people will not think about that so we have to promote it it just like +
> um generating funds for the church + as a source of revenue for the church because
> 5 + the church cannot survive without these monies coming in here and there +
> though people um wi- will make offering offering and other things like that + once
> in a year this is done + to generate more income for the church

Exercise 1

Listen to the extract and decide if the speaker has a rhotic or a non-rhotic accent.

Exercise 2

Mark the syllables you hear as stressed in the following phrases. (They are listed in order of occurrence in the Sequence.)

(a) so you have to set aside a special amount
(b) so we have to really promote it
(c) generating funds for the church
(d) as a source of revenue for the church
(e) once in a year this is done

Exercise 3

Listen to the way the speaker says the following (starting at line 5). How would you describe the overall intonation pattern?

 . . . the church cannot survive without these monies coming in here and there . . .

Sequence 2

In this short extract she is speaking about the style of dressing in Ghana.

1 one thing is that + our our costume + in Ghana we've adopted the European style
2 of dressing as well as ours + so we in both category whereby we can + when you
3 going to church you can put on suit whatever you want to + so we are used to using
4 our own + um form of dressing as well as what the Europeans brought us through
5 colon- colonialisation so . . .

Question 1

Some speakers of English have a palatal glide [j] before /uː/ and after the alveolar consonants [t, d, s, z, n, l] and the dental [θ] in their phonological system. Some examples are: 'tube', 'dune', 'assume', 'presume', 'newt', 'lewd' and 'enthuse'. In other words, they produce a consonant cluster before /uː/ instead of a single consonant: /tjuːb/, /djuːn/, /əsjuːm/, etc. Other speakers do not have this system, and will say /tuːb/, /duːn/, etc.

Listen to how the speaker says the words 'costume' and 'suit' – what system does she have?

Question 2

How would you transcribe her pronunciation of the following words or phrases:

- **(a)** one thing is that (line 1)
- **(b)** Ghana (line 1)
- **(c)** adopted (line 1)
- **(d)** category (line 2)
- **(e)** European (line 1)/Europeans (line 4)
- **(f)** our own form of dressing (line 4)
- **(g)** ours (line 2)
- **(h)** our (line 1)

Question 3

Listen to the speaker's use of pitch in the following comment on dress styles in Ghana. Try to sketch in her pattern of intonation on the staves above the words:

_____

_____

our costume   in Ghana we've adopted the European style of

_____

_____

dressing as well as ours

Sequence 3

Just before this next extract, the conversation had turned to the number of students on the course who have multilingual backgrounds. The speaker then describes how she and her sisters (who also both live in London) switch between their languages when they talk with each other.

for instance I speak two + Ghanaian languages + because I speak my mother's
language and my Daddy's language as well so I've got two of them + and for
instance if I'm speaking to my sisters we can + be- doing both code-switching here
and there + and one thing is that since + um we've got our + own language when
5 we speaking we just mix them up + we can speak the two um + indigenous
languages and bring in some English + and at times some few words in French +
which we do which we do which we do which we do I don't know but this is what
we've been doing all the time + (unintell . . . a rich mix) which we do so we'll be
talking + and especially when we say something and we don't want the (unintell)
10 other person around to know about it that's what we usually do + we'll be on the
phone talking and find us changing words here and there code-switching

Exercise 4

Question 1

Listen again to the following remark which starts at line 4, and decide which
words are given most emphasis by the speaker. How would you paraphrase the
meaning that she conveys by making these words prominent?

> . . . and one thing is that since em we've got our own language when we speaking
> we just mix them up . . .

Question 2

Describe the use of intonation in the following remark (starting at line 5), including the general direction of particular phrases – steadily rising or steadily falling
– as well as the choice of rising or falling pitch on particular words.

> . . . we can speak the two indigenous languages and bring in some English and at
> times some few words in French which we do which we do which we do which we
> do

Sequence 4

The two participants have been talking about traditional stories which, the
speaker says, are used to teach children about their culture and the code of
behaviour in their society. In this sequence she tells one of the traditional stories
involving a character in Ghanaian culture called Kweku-ananse, who is a spider.

Spider was invited to the mother-in-law's house + he went there and refused to eat
+ but what did he do + [laughs] he refused to eat because he just wanted- oh no
I've come into my mother-in-law's house I shouldn't eat I have to just be here
nicely + so he didn't eat meanwhile he was feeling very hungry + at the end of the
5   day + he went to steal some of of the food and put it + in his hat (ohh) so [she
laughs again] as he was going the thing started burning burning burning and so at
the end of the day he had to take the hat off + and everybody got to know oh after
all Kweku-ananse stole some food and put it on his head + instead of just saying I
want to eat instead of instead of him so here what it's saying is that you so – you
10 should be yourself + instead of trying to be what you are not

Exercise 5

Question 1

Some speakers of English have two forms of the article 'the'. A pronunciation
with [ði] will be used if the next word begins with a vowel, as in 'the intriguing
bit was the ending' [ði ɪntriːgɪŋ bɪt wɒz ði ɛndɪŋ]. The other will be a pronunciation with schwa if the next word begins with a consonant 'the best bit was the
beginning' [ðə bɛs(t) bɪt wɒz ðə bɪgɪnɪŋ]. Other speakers will use a pronunciation with schwa in **all** contexts.

Listen to the story of Kweku-ananse again. What system does this speaker
have? Then check the previous sequences for further examples to confirm your
analysis.

Question 2

Find all of the words in the story with each of the following diphthongs:

(a) /aɪ/   (b) /eɪ/   (c) /oʊ/   (d) /aʊ/

Question 3

What vowel does she have in 'burning'?

Question 4

Listen to the number of occasions where the speaker uses the preposition 'to'.
How many times does she use a pronunciation with schwa ([tə]), and how many
times do you hear a vowel with rounding [uː/ u or ʊ]?

✎ Question 5

Listen to each of the three times she said the word 'instead'. Are they identical?

✎ Question 6

Some speakers with language profiles similar to this speaker do not have a distinction between /iː/ and /ɪ/. Listen for these two vowels in the story of Kweku-ananse. Does this speaker have this distinction or not?

✎ Question 7

In some varieties of English, speakers have one labio-velar glide – the voiced one, /w/, in words with 'w-' or 'wh-' in the spelling. So the words 'which' and 'witch', 'whether' and 'weather', or 'whet' and 'wet' will all be pronounced with /w/. Speakers of other varieties will have the voiced glide in words spelled with 'w-' but the voiceless glide, /hw/, in words spelled with 'wh-'.

Listen to the story and decide which system the speaker has. To do this you will need to compare her pronunciation of the words 'what' and 'meanwhile', with that of 'was', and 'went' (twice).

✎ Question 8

Listen to the moral of the story, and mark the syllables that you hear as prominent or stressed. Then, think what other possible choices might have been made.

you should be yourself instead of trying to be what you are not

✎ Question 9

In her telling of the story, what intonation patterns does she use on the following tone units. Use lines drawn on the staves to represent the pitch movement.

_____

_____

(a) to the mother-in-law's house

_____

_____

(b) refused to eat

_____

_____

(c) but what did he do

_____

_____

(d) I have to just be here nicely

_____

_____

(e) in his hat

Tasks for extension or discussion

Using the transcript, write the story of Spider as it might appear in a collection of folktales. Make some recordings of people reading it aloud, and then analyse and compare their use of stress and intonation.

Looking back

In this unit we have worked on a range of features and gained practice in listening carefully to the pronunciation of particular sounds, to the placement of stressed syllables in an utterance, to the various forms a speaker has of the same word, and to the use of intonation.

Unit 8 Key and comments

EXERCISE 1

She has a non-rhotic accent. Many speakers with a non-rhotic accent have what is called **linking r**. This means that words **are** pronounced with an /r/ after the vowel when the **next** word begins with a vowel sound. For example, in 'car boot sale' the /r/ would not be pronounced at the end of 'car', but in the phrase 'car engine' it would be. In the case of this speaker, in 'more income', 'your offering', there is no 'linking r' sound, but in the phrase 'here and there . . .' there is. In 'offering', she does pronounce an /r/, but in the following words she does not have /r/: year/ your/ church/ source/ survive/ there/ other.

EXERCISE 2

(a) so you ′have to ′set a′side a ′special a′mount
(b) so we ′have to ′really pro ′mote it
(c) ′gener′ating ′funds for the ′church
(d) as a ′source of ′reve′nue for the ′church
(e) ′once in a ′year ′this is ′done

In both (a) and (b) two different listeners heard two different patterns. One listener heard 'so' as stressed in both, and the other did not hear 'so' as stressed in both. Locating stresses in spontaneous speech is certainly not straightforward.

EXERCISE 3

Her intonation steps steadily down from the word 'church' to the end, with each stressed syllable said on a high pitch, but successive stressed syllables slightly lower than each previous one. The pattern is something like this:

the church cannot survive without these monies coming in

here and there

EXERCISE 3 Question 1

She uses the glide: /kɒstjuːm/   /sjuːt/

The range of consonants /j/ may follow depends on the variety of English. Many varieties of North American English do not use /j/ following alveolars and /θ/, but do use it in words such as 'value' (/valjuː/), and 'penury' (/pɛnjuːri/), that is, after /l/ and /n/ in unaccented syllables. Some British English varieties, such as Cockney, have a similar system, whereas other varieties, such as RP, use a /j/ glide following all of the alveolars and /θ/. (See Davenport and Hannahs (1998: 35).)

EXERCISE 3 **Question 2**

(a) wɒnθɪnɪz ðat **(b)** gɑnɑ **(c)** adɔːptɛd **(d)** katəgɔri
(e) juroʊpiən(z) **(f)** ɑːoʊn fɔːm əv drɛsɪn **(g)** aʊwəz **(h)** aʊə

Note how her pronunciation of 'our' can vary.

EXERCISE 3 **Question 3**

our costume   in Ghana we've adopted the European style of

dressing as well as ours

In discussing the intonation of Englishes used in West Africa, J. C. Wells observes the following: 'the common African pattern is a succession of jumps from high to low and back to (not quite so) high and then to low again, as "stressed" and "unstressed" syllables alternate' (1982: 643). This statement seems to describe quite well the intonation here and in the phrase above in Exercise 3.

EXERCISE 4 **Question 1**

The words 'since', 'own', 'got' and 'language' are all very prominent. We might give the following paraphrase: our behaviour is determined by the fact that we have our own language – if we didn't, then we would behave differently. The prominence on 'since' conveys the central idea of causality, and that on the words 'own language' conveys the contrast between Akan and the language spoken where they both are living, English.

EXERCISE 4 **Question 2**

we can speak the two indigenous languages and bring in some

English and at times some few words in French

Of note here is how after the word 'and' her pitch steadily moves upwards, and then is at a high point on 'in' from which it falls sharply on 'French' (a 'high fall'). There are fall–rises on 'language' and 'English'. These fall-rises are probably showing non-finality – her list of their languages is not finished. The fall on 'French' could be showing finality ('This is the last item in the list.') and the *high* fall might show that she is informing her listener of something she wants the listener to pay particular attention to. Since she knows that her listener knows that French is the language that she and her sister are least fluent in, she may also be marking this information as 'unexpected'.

EXERCISE 5 Question 1

She uses the pronunciation with schwa except in the first part of the phrase 'at the end of the day'. So, she seems to have the system of 'the' pronounced with schwa except before a following vowel in the next word. Interestingly, though, in Sequence 3, where we would expect /ðiː/ in the phrase 'we don't want **the other** person around to know about it' (lines 9–10) she does not use /iː/ but a lower shorter vowel in the region of /ɛ/. In Sequence 2, where she says 'the Europeans' she also uses this vowel.

EXERCISE 5 Question 2

/aɪ/ spider invited nicely meanwhile trying
/eɪ/ day saying take   /aʊ/ house
/oʊ/ stole going no know

EXERCISE 5 Question 3

The vowel in 'burning' is /ɛː/. It is the long vowel before /r/ that is characteristic of RP. Other words that would have this vowel are 'bird', 'work', or 'fern'.

EXERCISE 5 Question 4

She seems not to use schwa, but a high back vowel with rounding /uː/, /u/, or /ʊ/. In most cases, the vowel she uses is not very long, so we could choose either [tu] or [tʊ] to transcribe her pronunciation.

EXERCISE 5 Question 5

No. On the first two occasions she stresses the first syllable, but the third time she says it she seems to stress the second syllable as well.

EXERCISE 5 Question 6

Yes, she does have the two vowel phonemes /iː/ and /ɪ/.

EXERCISE 5 Question 7

She has both voiced and voiceless glides. The voiceless one is used in 'what' and 'meanwhile'. The easiest to hear of the voiceless pronunciations is the one in 'mean**wh**ile'.

EXERCISE 5 Question 8

you 'should 'be your'self in'stead of 'trying to 'be 'what you are 'not.

EXERCISE 5 Question 9

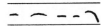

(a) to the mother-in-law's house

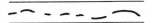

(b) refused to eat

(c) but what did he do

(d) I have to just be here nicely

(e) in his hat

Where do babies get their food from?

Preview

English is spoken as an additional language by people all over the world. Many of these speakers will use their English in talking to native speakers of English; many others will use it when speaking to other non-native speakers. Speakers of English as an additional language may use their communication skills in primarily one context or setting, perhaps in their working lives, or in many different settings, for example, academic study, work, talking with friends, travel, etc. It can therefore be difficult to predict what skills they need: writing, speaking, formal negotiation skills, informal conversational skills, and so on. Depending on the context in which they are using their English skills, speakers may feel more or less at ease or confident. In this unit we will analyse a speaker's pronunciation in three different speaking tasks.

Background

In this recording you will hear two speakers whose first language is Brazilian Portuguese. At the time of recording both were living in London. One of them was a student on a university course, and was studying English and Linguistics. For one of her projects, she asked one of her friends to help her by being tape-recorded reading aloud and speaking in English. Her friend agreed, and they set up the recording session in her home. The student decided she should choose a reading passage and topic that was familiar and relevant to her 'subject', and since her friend had just had her third child, she chose a short passage on breast-feeding for her to read aloud. She then planned to ask her to retell the content of the passage in her own words, and to have a short informal chat about the topic.

The first sequence is the reading aloud task. The title was 'Where do babies get their food from?'

Sequence I

eh where do babies get their + eh where do babies get their food from? Human babies, kittens, and puppies can get all the food they need to grow in the first few months from their mother's breast. Many children do not realise this and have never seen a child fed from the breast. Others think that breast-feeding comes first
5   and later bottle-feeding. They don't realise they are used as alter- alternatives. This picture is changing as the breast versus bottle argument is now getting a lot of publicity. When children see a baby breast-fed they are usually fascinated and have lots of questions to ask. 'Doesn't he get hungry drinking only milk?' You may find that now that children are becoming more aware of breast-feeding you will be
10 asked more questions about it.

Exercise I

Question 1

There are several two-syllable words in the passage. Listen to the stress pattern used by the speaker on these words, and decide if she places the main accent on the same syllable as natives speakers of English do.

(a) babies **(b)** human **(c)** kittens **(d)** puppies **(e)** mother's **(f)** children **(g)** never **(h)** others **(i)** later **(j)** bottle **(k)** picture **(l)** changing **(m)** versus **(n)** bottle **(o)** getting **(p)** breast-fed **(q)** questions **(r)** hungry **(s)** drinking **(t)** only **(u)** aware **(v)** about

Question 2

Now listen to her pronunciation of the following three- and four-syllable words, and note the stress pattern.

(a) realise (occurs twice) **(b)** breast-feeding (occurs twice) **(c)** alternatives **(d)** argument **(e)** publicity **(f)** usually **(g)** fascinated

Exercise 2

The vowel systems of English and Brazilian Portuguese are very different. Whereas English has between from about 12 to 23 vowel phonemes, depending on the accent, Brazilian Portuguese has a system with seven vowel phonemes. They are as follows:

/i/ close front
/e/ half close front
/ɛ/ half low front
/a/ low
/u/ high back round
/o/ half close back
/ɔ/ half low back

Question 1

In English there are two vowel phonemes in the close front/high front area of the 'vowel space': /iː/ as in 'feet' and /ɪ/ as in 'fit'. As we see from the Brazilian system, there is one close front/high front vowel. Listen to her pronunciation of the words in the passage in which /i/ and /ɪ/ occur. Transcribe these words to show the vowel sound she is using.

Words with /i/	Words with /ɪ/	
need line 2	kittens line 2	children lines 3/9
seen line 4		
breast-feeding line 4	this lines 3/5	think line 4
see line 7	breast-feeding line 4	picture line 6
he line 8	is line 6	
be line 9	fascinated line 7	drinking line 8
	milk line 8	
	will line 9	it line 10

Question 2

Brazilian Portuguese does not use the vowel /ʌ/ as in 'fun'. Find the words in the passage with this vowel, then listen to her pronunciation and decide whether she uses this vowel or not. If she uses another vowel, try to decide how to transcribe it.

The words are: puppies months mother's publicity hungry becoming others comes.

Question 3

Brazilian Portuguese has no diphthongs in its vowel system as does English. From this comparison of the two systems, that of the learner's native language and that of the 'target' language, we might expect her to have difficulty in pronouncing words with the English diphthongs. Look through the passage to identify words with the following diphthongs, and then listen to her pronunciation.

/eɪ/ as in 'play'   /aɪ/ 'eye'   /oʊ/ 'go'   /aʊ/ 'now'

Question 4

The two vowel systems share a common vowel in /ɛ/ as in 'bed'. Since this would seem to require on her part no other process than a simple recognition of this familiar vowel in the English system, we could expect her pronunciation of words with /ɛ/ to match that of English speakers perfectly. Look for words with /ɛ/ and check if this seems to be the case.

Exercise 3

The consonant systems of English and Brazilian Portuguese are much more similar than the vowel systems are. There are a few differences though. Portuguese has a larger system of nasal sounds than English: as well as having bi-labial, alveolar and velar nasals, it also has a palatal nasal and a labio-velar nasal. One consonant that English uses that Brazilian Portuguese does not use is the /h/. As we have seen, this occurs in syllable initial position in most varieties of English in words such as 'heat' and 'have', and can best be described as a period of voicelessness before the vowel sound. When it occurs between vowels, as in 'ahead' or 'behave' it can be voiced (see Unit 1).

Question 1

Listen to how the speaker reads the following sections of the passage. How would you describe her pronunciation of the words with initial /h/?

(a) and have never seen a child fed from the breast lines 3–4
(b) and have lots of questions to ask lines 7–8
(c) doesn't he get hungry drinking only milk line 8

Question 2

The Brazilian consonant system does not use the dental fricatives that occur in the English system, i.e. the voiceless dental fricative, /θ/, as in 'thick' and the voiced one, /ð/, as in 'the' or 'those'. Listen to her pronunciation of the following words with these sounds, and try to transcribe what you hear. (The phrases are listed in order of occurrence.)

(a) get **th**eir food from
(b) all **the** food **th**ey need
(c) in **the** first few mon**th**s
(d) from **th**eir mo**th**er's breast
(e) do not realise **th**is
(f) fed from **the** breast
(g) o**th**ers **th**ink **th**at
(h) **th**ey don't realise **th**ey are used
(i) **the** breast versus bottle argument
(j) **th**ey are usually fascinated
(k) **th**at now **th**at children are becoming

Question 3

There are several words which begin with the voiceless bi-labial plosive /p/ in the passage. Brazilian Portuguese has the same set of six plosives that English does: /p/, /b/, /t/, /d/, /k/ and /g/. Listen to her pronunciation of the words with the voiced and voiceless bi-labial plosives and describe her pronunciation of these two plosives. (There are several occurrences of some of these words, so check if her pronunciation seems to be consistent.)

Words with /p/	Words with /b/
puppies line 2	babies/baby lines 1/2/7
picture line 6	breast/breast-feeding lines 3/4/6/7/9
publicity line 7	bottle lines 5/6
	becoming line 9
	be line 9

Question 4

As we have seen above, both English and Portuguese share the two alveolar plosives, /t/ and /d/. The /d/ occurs a few times in the passage at the beginning of words, as in 'do'/'doesn't' and 'drinking', and, as one might expect, there is no difference between her pronunciation and that of an English speaker. The sound also occurs several times at the end of words, as in 'need' and 'food' and also medially, as in the word 'feeding'.

Listen to her pronunciation of /d/ in these positions. You will notice that word final and medial position don't seem to be as 'straightforward' as initial. Try to describe what you hear.

Word final /d/	Medial /d/
get their foo**d** from line 1	later bottle-fee**d**ing line 5
kittens an**d** puppies line 2	
all the foo**d** they line 2	that breast-fee**d**ing line 4
they nee**d** to grow line 2	many chil**d**ren line 3
an**d** have never seen line 3	
fe**d** from the breast line 4	of breast-fee**d**ing line 9
use**d** as alternatives line 5	
see a baby breast-fe**d** they are line 7	
usually fascinate**d** an**d** have line 7	
you may fin**d** that lines 8–9	

Exercise 4

As we have seen, the consonant systems of Brazilian and English are very similar. Given that this is the case, one would think that the following words would be 'simple' for the speaker to pronounce as they contain only consonant sounds that are 'familiar' to her: 'first', 'lots', 'ask' and 'milk'. (These are also very common words and therefore high frequency.) But you will have noticed in listening to the passage that this seems not to be the case.

Question 1

Analyse these words in terms of the sequences of vowels and consonants (that is, do they have single consonants preceding or following vowels, or consonant clusters). Then listen to her pronunciation and do a transcription.

Question 2

What explanation might there be for the way she pronounces these words?

After she had finished reading the story aloud, she was asked to retell it in her own words. Listen to her retelling. In the transcript, 'S' stands for the subject, and 'R' stands for the 'researcher'. At one point you can hear the voice of one of her children in the background. In fact, it sounds as if the child has picked up the paper and is herself reading aloud, like her mother just has!

R: that's very good   can you tell me now the story again
S: yes I can   eh human babies and the cats' babies or dogs' babies they
R: what is the story about   is it about + breast-feeding
5 **S:**   ahh   breast-feeding the animals and the human + being and this kind of babies humans cats and dogs they are usually breast-fed + breast-feeding + then they get all they need from their mother's milk + eh a lot of children doesn't realise eh this + and the importance of breast-feeding and many of
10   them have never seen a baby breast-fed + when(?) they if they see a baby + (R: being) being fed fed they ask a lot of questions about + eh how do the babies get all they need from only the mommy's milk
R: you mean there are questions about + is it (unintell)
15 **S:** yes I think it is a natural curiosity from the children and they admire baby having milk from mothers

E x e r c i s e   5

Question 1

Identify some points of similarity between the pronunciation of the speaker when she is reading aloud, and when she is re-telling the text. Because she is bound to use some of the exact words or phrases from the passage, you will be able to compare these across the two sequences. Here are some particular points to investigate, based on the four exercises in the unit so far.

1 /i/ versus /ɪ/
2 use of /h/
3 dental fricatives /θ/ and /ð/

4 words with consonant clusters, e.g. 'first' 'milk'
5 stress pattern in words with three or more syllables
6 word final /t/ and /d/
7 the pronunciation of /d/ in 'breast-feeding'

Sequence 3

The retelling task merges into a period of spontaneous talk on the subject after the researcher asks her about her personal opinion about breast-feeding. (The researcher's choice of passage seems to indeed have been ideal, because her friend tells of her own older children's reaction to seeing the baby breast-fed.)

Before you look at the transcript below, you might want to listen and try to make your own transcript. This could help to indicate if there are any features of her pronunciation which might cause problems of intelligibility for her listeners.

R: and what is your personal opinion about breast-feeding
S: breast-feeding oh I think it's the best thing + the best for the baby + and for the mother
R: and do you feel nice breast-feeding your little baby
5 **S:** oh yes I feel very happy
R: how is he getting on
S: oh he's very well he's developing + nicely and I hope to feed him at least two months
R: oh are you
10 **S:** yes [laugh]
R: does he get much I mean bad bad pains or
S: no he's nice he sleeps (?) nicely even during the night he never cries and he has a little colic and he's not a too mingy (?) baby I think it because he's breast-fed
15 **R:** oh that's that sounds nice + how how are your other children getting on with the baby + are they satisfied with the little one
S: yes they are very happy   ah   eh talking about breast-feeding + for the first time that they saw me feeding the baby oh they were very curious about the baby 'mommy why he must have milk from you?'
20 'is he eat you' [both laugh] I tried to explain them that when they were baby they were breast-fed as well as the little one and now it's nothing news for them + they are used to

R: I see + does he accept well the bottle + I mean do you feed him
from the bottle

25 **S:** ah   once eh (?) I felt that I was short of milk + then I prepare just
a little milk in the bottle for him + oh it was a great struggle to eh
(R: to try) to try + he did not want to suck the bottle he refused he
turned over his head (R: oh) but as he was very hungry he tried to
suck but he had very little + I think he prefer breast-feeding

Question 2

How does her pronunciation in this sequence compare with her reading aloud
and her retelling of the passage? Look again at the list of points in Question 1 to
guide you in your analysis.

Question 3

In your view, what features seem to be what we might call 'stable' features of
her pronunciation of English, and which features seem to be more variable? Bear
in mind that reading aloud and retelling from memory what you have read, especially while you are being tape-recorded, are not everyday activities for most
people, so these could be tasks which cause feelings of pressure or self-
consciousness.

Looking back

In this unit we have seen clearly how a comparison of the sound systems of two
languages can shed light on the pronunciation of users of English as an additional language. We have seen also that their pronunciation can vary according
to task and situation.

Tasks for consolidation or discussion

If the speaker wanted to know what aspects of her pronunciation were most
important for her to try to change, how would you answer?

Judging from your analysis of the speaker's performance on these three
speaking tasks, what do you think are the implications for the assessment and
analysis of the pronunciation of non-native speakers?

Listen to the pronunciation of the researcher and analyse the extent to which her pronunciation seems to be influenced by the system of her native language.

Unit 9 Key and comments

EXERCISE 1 Question 1

In all of the words she uses the same stress pattern as native speakers would.

EXERCISE 1 Question 2

(a) 'realise' is pronounced as a three-syllable word with stress on the final syllable.
(b) She seems to put a stronger stress on the second part of this compound than a native speaker probably would.
(c) 'alternatives' has this pattern: ˈal terˈna tives. She also uses a full vowel [eː] in the third syllable instead of schwa. This pattern is quite different from al ˈter na tives, with the main stress on the second syllable.
(d) 'argument' and **(e)** 'publicity' are given the same pattern as native speakers would.
(f) 'usually' is pronounced with four syllables with the main stress on the first. In most contexts, this would be pronounced with three /ˈjuːʒəli/ by native speakers.
(g) 'fascinated' receives the main stress on the third syllable [fasɪˈneɪtəd] in her pronunciation, contrasting with main stress on the first, with another stress on the third [ˈfasɪˈneɪtəd] by native speakers.

EXERCISE 2 Question 1

She has the /iː/ vowel in the words in the left-hand column, as one would expect, but in words with /ɪ/ there is some variation. In particular, 'kittens', 'this', 'think', 'picture' and 'is' have an /iː/ vowel instead of /ɪ/.

EXERCISE 2 Question 2

The words 'publicity', 'hungry', 'becoming', 'others' and 'comes' have an /ʌ/. But the words 'puppies', 'months' 'mother's' have a vowel which seems to be a bit lower, in the region of /ɑ/.

EXERCISE 2 Question 3

Even though her first language has no diphthongs, she pronounces these with apparent ease. An example for each is 'babies' /eɪ/, 'realise' /aɪ/, 'grow' /oʊ/ although this sounds more like a long /o:/, and 'now' /aʊ/.

EXERCISE 2 Question 4

As expected, words like 'get', 'many' and 'never' are clearly pronounced with the /ɛ/ vowel.

EXERCISE 3 Question 1

In all the examples there are many occurrences of /h/ which is not a period of voicelessness before the vowel, but pronounced as a fricative. A possible choice is /x/, the symbol for the voiceless velar fricative.

EXERCISE 3 Question 2

In pronouncing grammatical words, such as 'the', 'their', 'they', 'this' and 'that', which all have the voiced dental fricative /ð/, she seems to substitute a voiced alveolar plosive, /d/. In (c) she deletes the sound completely, producing a word with two consonants at the end instead of three /mɑns/. Note, however, that native speakers also often use this pronunciation in spontaneous speech, and would probably only say 'months' with three consonants in formal speaking situations, e.g. reading aloud a list of words. In pronouncing (d) 'mother's' and (g) 'others' she uses a /d/. In the word 'think' (g) she uses a /t/. Notice the pattern in her substitutions: /d/, a voiced alveolar plosive is used as a substitute for the **voiced** dental fricative, and /t/, the voiceless alveolar plosive is used as a substitute for the voiceless dental fricative. So she uses a consonant sound that matches the voicing of the sound in these words, and a consonant that is close to the place of articulation.

EXERCISE 3 Question 3

In the three words with /p/ she uses very weak aspiration, that is, the voicing for the following vowel begins much sooner after the plosive is produced when compared with native English speakers. One doesn't hear the sound of a puff of air as the plosive is released (*see* Unit 1). In fact, to the English ear, the first sound of 'puppies' sounds more like a /b/ than a /p/.

<u>Question 4</u>

In the word 'feeding' the /d/ sounds like a /dʒ/. This may seem odd, but one explanation is that perhaps in Portuguese, when a /d/ occurs next to the vowel /i:/ it is influenced by that vowel. In this word the /d/ is 'surrounded' by two high front vowels. Since high front vowels are made with the tongue near the hard palate, the alveolar consonant is modified to a palatal consonant, and /dʒ/ is a palato-alveolar consonant. (This process of modification of a sound to become more **similar** to the sounds near it is termed 'as**simila**tion'.)

When a word has a final /d/ sound, she inserts a short vowel after it. So we could transcribe this as [fu:də] or [ni:də]. There are two cases when this isn't so apparent: at line 5 in the phrase 'used as' and in line 7, on the word 'fascinated'. One explanation could be that in both of these cases, the next word begins with a vowel sound, unlike all the other cases when a consonant sound follows next. We could speculate that in her native language sequences of consonant–consonant, or 'abutting consonants' are not usual; the normal pattern is consonant–vowel–consonant. When we listen carefully to these two 'more English sounding examples' we can see that her pronunciation is still different from what a native English speaker would produce. English speakers would link the final /d/ to the vowel very smoothly. This could be represented with the transcription [ju:zdaz] or [ju:zdəz]. She doesn't use this linking.

<u>Question 1</u>

'first'   CVCCC   (or CVCC for non-rhotic accents)   [fərsti]
'lots'   CVCC   [lɔtɪs]
'ask'   VCC   [aski]
'milk'   CVCC   [milki]   (This sounds like the adjective 'milky'!)

<u>Question 2</u>

To explain this, we might appeal again to the syllable structure of her native language. Perhaps clusters of consonants are very infrequent and not part of the phonological pattern of Brazilian Portuguese, so she tries to break these apart when they occur in English words by either inserting a vowel between two consonants as in [lɔtɪs] or adding a vowel at the end of the word, so she is changing the structure of word. For example, 'ask' becomes VC–CV and 'milk' becomes CVC–CV.

EXERCISE 5 <u>Question 1</u>

1 In words like 'this' lines 6, 9 and 'think' line 15 she uses /iː/.

2 She uses friction on /h/ although at times it is not so strong, as in line 10 'have never seen' and line 12 'how do'.

3 She replaces /d/ for the dental fricatives on grammatical words, but in the case of 'mother' at lines 8 and 16 she uses a fricative.

4 An interesting case is the word 'milk'. When she says it at line 8 she adds a vowel at the end, but at lines 13 and 16 she does not. On 'ask' at line 11, she also does not add a vowel.

5 The words 'importance', 'natural curiosity' and 'admire' all have the stress patterns English speakers would use.

6 She adds a vowel on 'breast-fed' at line 7, 'need' at line 8, 'fed' at line 11, and 'get' at line 12. But 'kind of' at line 6 does not have a vowel added. Note that the next word begins with a vowel.

7 On both occurrences of this word, the /d/ is pronounced as /dʒ/.

EXERCISE 5 <u>Question 2</u>

1 The word 'think' at line 14 has /iː/ but 'thing' at line 2 does not.

2 Her initial /h/ sounds seems very fricative-like in many cases as in 'hope' at line 7 and 'happy' at line 17, and 'hungry' line 28, but some of the pronunciations of the word 'he' do not have much friction, for example at line 7.

3 The word 'think' line 29 has /t/, but several of the occurrences of 'the' and 'they', 'that' and 'thing' are pronounced with fricatives, e.g. 'the best thing' line 2; 'the first time that they' line 18.

4 She does not insert vowels to break up consonant clusters as in 'best' line 2 or 'least' line 8, nor does she add a vowel to the word 'milk' on the three occasions she says it at lines 19, 25 and 26. She does add a vowel to the word 'must' at line 19.

5 The word 'developing' at line 7 is pronounced in an 'English' way.

6 The addition of a schwa vowel after word-final /t/ and /d/ is not nearly so apparent here. It does occur at 'breast-fed' line 21, and at line 28 on 'head'.

7 Each time she says this word in this sequence she uses /d/.

EXERCISE 5 <u>Question 3</u>

The substitution of plosives for the dental fricatives and the use of a fricative for /h/ seem to be stable features, but we have seen variation in both of these areas in the spontaneous speech sequences. The insertion of vowels to break up consonant clusters persists in all of the speaking tasks, but in the reading aloud they seem to be much more striking. The same could be said of the insertion of vowels after word final /t/ and /d/. The pronunciation of 'breast-fee**d**ing' is a case where we could speculate that by the end of the recording being made, she has said this word several times, and has heard her Portuguese friend say it (without using a /dʒ/) several times. Perhaps we are witnessing her learning not to use assimilation here!

Note that when she pronounces words with a sequence of /tr-/ or /dr-/, as in 'try' or 'drinking' in the recording, she uses a plosive then a trilled 'r', as opposed to the affricates that many native English speakers would use. However, this does not seem to affect the intelligibility of these words.

There was once a little princess

Preview

The recordings in this unit will be used to examine the way that some pronunciation features are used not as part of the identity of a word, but as a response to certain expressive needs. They will also be used to investigate the pronunciation of speakers of English as an additional language. It is useful to be able to compare and contrast the pronunciation of different speakers saying the same thing, but the only way to do this in many cases is to ask several different people to read aloud the same written text.

Background

For the majority of people, reading a text aloud is a rarely performed activity. It is probably most frequently done in educational settings as a learning exercise, or as a test to allow the teacher to check on performance. Teachers themselves may read aloud to their pupils for many reasons – in order to present a model, as part of a dictation or comprehension exercise, or for the enjoyment of a story. Teachers are therefore quite comfortable with the task of reading aloud.

Outside of educational institutions, people may occasionally read short bits of text aloud to others, from a newspaper, or set of instructions, or from a guide-book when on holiday. However, for adults, there is one setting in which it seems very natural to read aloud, and where the experience is a very rewarding and warmly personal one – reading a story to a young child.

Reading to young children seems to be a specific type of 'event'. Just as there are characteristic ways of talking to young children, when reading to young children, adults manipulate features of their pronunciation.

Exercise I

Listen to Sequence 1. The speaker was asked to read the first part of a story, *The Princess and the Goblin*, by George MacDonald, as if she were reading it aloud to a six- or seven-year-old child.

Sequences 1–5

> There was once a little princess whose father was king over a great country full of mountains and valleys. His palace was built upon one of the mountains, and was very grand and beautiful. The princess, whose name was Irene, was born there, but she was sent soon after her birth, because her mother was not very strong, to be brought up by country people in a large house, half castle, half farmhouse, on the side of another mountain.

Question 1

Make a list of some of the features that the speaker uses which you think distinguishes this reading as designed for children.

Question 2

Now listen to Sequence 2, a more neutral reading by the same adult. She was asked to read aloud as if her listeners were other adults. What differences are there between the two readings?

Exercise 2

Sequences 3, 4 and 5 are also readings aloud of the same text, but these were done by speakers of English as an additional language. They were all advanced learners of English in their early twenties, and were asked to make a recording of the beginning of the story and imagine that they were reading aloud to a young child.

Question 1

Listen to the three readings. To what extent do these show the typical features of reading aloud to young children? Which reader do you think comes closest to the way the adult read the story in Sequence 1?

Question 2

As well as having some of the typical features of 'fairy tales' (a royal family, grand palaces and a goblin), the story has one of the typical formulaic openings of the fairy story: 'there was once . . .'. Compare the delivery of this opening by the native speaker in Sequence 1 with those used by the three non-native readers, that is:

(a) which word or words are stressed or unstressed
(b) what vowel is used in the word 'was'
(c) does the speaker start at a high, mid, or low point in his or her pitch range
(d) what is the overall shape of the pitch movement?

Exercise 3

The third sentence of the extract from the story is 45 words long and very complex in structure. It has two main parts linked by 'but'. The first main clause ('The princess was born there . . .') has a relative clause ('. . . whose name was Irene . . .'). The second main clause (' . . . She was sent soon after her birth . . .) has a reason clause (' . . . because her mother was not very strong . . .'). The last part of this sentence has four phrases: '. . . by country people . . . in a large house . . . on the side . . . of another mountain.' The word 'house' is described by two phrases ('. . . half castle, half farmhouse'). One indication of how complex this sentence is, is that it has eight commas.

When people read aloud they are to some extent influenced by the punctuation they see in the written text.

Question 1

Do all the readers pause at each comma? Do any of them use pause at other points in the sentence?

Question 2

For each of the readings, identify whether the reader uses falling or rising tones on the words which *precede* the commas in the text.

	1	2	3	4	5
princess					
Irene					
there					
birth					
strong					
people					
house					
castle					
farmhouse					

Exercise 4

Listen again to the reading in Sequence 3. Her first language is Japanese.

Question 1

How would you transcribe the vowel sounds she uses in each syllable of these two-syllable words:

Sentence 1: **(a)** princess   **(b)** mountains
Sentence 2: **(c)** upon   **(d)** mountains
Sentence 3: **(e)** mother   **(f)** people   **(g)** mountain

Question 2

Native speakers of English would use the same initial consonant sound in the words 'whose' (Sentences 1 and 3), 'his' (2), 'her' (2), 'house' (3), 'half' (twice in 3). This sound would be transcribed as /h/ and would be produced as a voiceless onset to the following vowel. Does the Japanese speaker use /h/ in each of these words?

Question 3

How would you transcribe her pronunciation of these phrases:

(a) but she was sent soon after her birth
(b) was built upon
(c) to be brought up

Question 4

Japanese speakers who learn English must concentrate carefully on their pronunciation of the two liquids /l/ and /r/. In English, these two sounds belong to separate phonemes, that is, they are sounds which make a difference to the meanings of words. There are many pairs of words in English which are distinguished only by these two consonants: 'low' and 'row', 'lake' and 'rake', 'berry' and 'belly', and so on. As we have seen, in articulatory terms, the difference between these two consonant sounds lies in the position of the sides of the tongue against the upper molars for /r/ plus a groove down the centre of the tongue, whereas for /l/ there is contact between tip of the tongue and the alveolar ridge, with the sides of the tongue lowered.

These two sounds are used in Japanese, but they do not make a difference to the identity of a word; in fact, they are simply variants of one another – a speaker can use either sound and the word will be heard on each occasion by other Japanese ears as the same word. They are **allophones** of the same phoneme.

Listen to the speaker's pronunciation of the following words: do they sound more like an English /l/ or more like an /r/ to you? (They are listed in order of occurrence.)

(a) litt<u>l</u>e   **(b)** whose fathe<u>r</u> was   **(c)** ove<u>r</u> a great country
(d) fu<u>ll</u> of mountains and va<u>ll</u>eys   **(e)** pa<u>l</u>ace   **(f)** ve<u>r</u>y
(g) I<u>r</u>ene   **(h)** the<u>r</u>e   **(i)** afte<u>r</u> her   **(j)** anothe<u>r</u> mountain

Question 5

All of the words in the above list occur in final or medial position in the word. Now listen to words with /l/ or /r/ together with another consonant, or following a vowel.

(a) p<u>r</u>incess   **(b)** g<u>r</u>eat   **(c)** count<u>r</u>y   **(d)** g<u>r</u>and
(e) bo<u>r</u>n   **(f)** bi<u>r</u>th   **(g)** st<u>r</u>ong   **(h)** b<u>r</u>ought   **(i)** count<u>r</u>y
(j) la<u>r</u>ge   **(k)** fa<u>r</u>mhouse

Is there any pattern in her production of the /r/ sounds, or does it seem to be random (sometimes more like English /l/, sometimes more like an English-sounding /r/)?

Exercise 5

Listen to the reading by the speaker in Sequence 4. Her first language is Italian.

Question 1

How does this speaker pronounce the words with initial /h/? Use the list above given in Exercise 4 Question 2.

Question 2

Listen to the following phrases. How would you transcribe them?

(a) his palace was built upon
(b) the princess whose name was Irene
(c) but she was sent soon after her birth
(d) because her mother was not very strong

Question 3

Can you think of a reason why this speaker might be inserting a schwa so frequently when she reads aloud in English?

Question 4

What vowels does the speaker use in the following words?

(a) little   **(b)** the three occurrences of 'mountain(s)'
(c) beautiful   **(d)** because

Question 5

Does this speaker have a rhotic accent when she speaks English?
    We have seen that one characteristic of English pronunciation is that many two-syllable words will have one syllable which is stressed and one that is pronounced weakly. For speakers of English, pronouncing polysyllabic words involves giving different energy to syllables. These patterns are of course unconscious and automatic, but they are a key part of English pronunciation. The mental dictionary of every English speaker contains this information about word stress patterns, and speakers know when to carry out a process of 'weakening' or 'neutralization' of the vowel in a non-prominent syllable. They use a central vowel, schwa, or [ɪ] as in 'bit'.

Question 6

Listen to the speaker's pronunciation of these two-syllable words. Does she carry out this process of weakening or not?

(a) princess   **(b)** mountains (3 occurrences)
(c) beautiful

Exercise 6

Listen again to the reading in Sequence 5. His first language is Spanish.

Question 1

Speakers of English with a Spanish language background must concentrate carefully on the pronunciation of the labial consonants in the English sound system. Spanish has a voiced bi-labial fricative /β/. This sound is similar to /b/ in English, in that it is bi-labial and voiced, but it is dissimilar in that /b/ is a plosive and /β/ is a fricative. Spanish /β/ is similar to English /v/ – both are voiced and both are fricatives. But for /v/ the lower front teeth touch the upper lip; for /β/ the upper and lower lips come close together but the teeth are not involved in producing the sound. The following table sums up these contrasts:

	/b/	/v/	/β/
labio-dental	no	yes	no
bi-labial	yes	no	yes
voiced	yes	yes	yes
plosive	yes	no	no
fricative	no	yes	yes

Listen to the following words – in each case, does the speaker's /b/ match English /b/, i.e., is it a voiced, bi-labial plosive? (Words are in order of occurrence.)

(a) built   **(b)** beautiful   **(c)** born
(d) but   **(e)** birth   **(f)** because   **(g)** brought
(h) by

Question 2

There is no vowel similar to /ʌ/ in Spanish, so Spanish speakers of English sometimes use a substitute vowel. Listen to the following words. If you think the speaker is using a substitution strategy, what vowel is being used?

(a) country   **(b)** one   **(c)** mother   **(d)** country   **(e)** another

Exercise 7

The passage contains the word 'mountain(s)' three times. The first occurrence is in the first sentence. Someone reading the story aloud will convey through their use of intonation that this is 'new' information for the listener. The word occurs for a second time in the second sentence, but here, the focus could be said to have shifted to 'one' and away from 'mountains', so speakers may foreground 'one' and not 'mountains', which is treated as 'given' or 'old' information. When the word occurs in the third sentence, the information we are given is that the princess was brought up in a house on a different mountain from the one her father's palace is on. Someone reading the story aloud may use the features of pitch, volume, vowel length, and so on to convey this contrast between one mountain and another.

   Listen to both readings by the adult native English speaker to see how this process of 'highlighting' is used. Then listen to the readings by the Japanese, Italian and Spanish speakers to see if they do the same thing. The phrases in which 'mountain(s)' occur are listed below. You can use the following table to make a note of your observations.

	Japanese	Italian	Spanish
full of mountains			
one of the mountains			
another mountain			

Looking back

We have used this text read aloud to investigate how **paralinguistic features** are used when speaking in a particular situation to a particular type of listener. Speakers have a large repertoire of pronunciation. A comparison of the three speakers of English as an additional language has provided another opportunity to see how two sound systems interact in bilingual speakers.

Tasks for extension or discussion

If you were the teacher of these Japanese, Italian and Spanish speakers, and they wanted to work together and help each other on their pronunciation, which areas would you recommend that they help each other with?

Do any of these speakers share pronunciation features with the speaker of Brazilian Portuguese (Unit 9)?

Select any of the three non-native speaker readings and attempt a complete transcription of the whole passage. Suggested transcriptions are included at the end of the Key and Comments section.

Unit 10 Key and comments

EXERCISE 1 Questions 1 and 2

Some of the features include: a slightly slower speed of delivery, more frequent and slightly longer pauses, a special voice quality, the use of vowel lengthening, a lower volume, and more extreme pitch fluctuation. The reading for children by this speaker seems to use all of these features except lower volume. Note her use of high falls on the words 'born', 'sent', 'country', 'farmhouse' and the extended fall-rise on the word 'princess' in the third sentence.

EXERCISE 2 Question 1

The reading by the male speaker seems to come closest to this style. Although we have no neutral reading for comparison, the vowels in the words 'great', 'mountains', 'valleys', 'palace', 'grand', 'another' sound very long. He also uses a whispery voice quality, conveying a feeling of intimacy.

Question 2

READING 3

(a) the three words receive equal stress

(b) wɒz

(c) she starts at mid pitch

(d) the overall direction is falling

READING 4

(a) there is more stress on both 'was' and 'once'

(b) wɒzə

(c) she starts on mid pitch

(d) two slight falls, one on 'was' and one on 'once'

READING 5

(a) there is more stress on 'once'

(b) wɒz

(c) he starts at mid pitch
(d) a falling then a rising pattern

EXERCISE 3 <u>Question 1</u>

READER 3
She pauses after the following words: princess king valleys palace upon beautiful princess Irene there soon birth strong up people house farmhouse.

READER 4
Pauses after: princess mountains beautiful princess Irene there birth strong house farmhouse.

READER 5
Pauses after: princess valleys palace mountains beautiful princess Irene there soon birth strong brought people house castle farmhouse side.

There are only a few instances where the three non-native readers do not pause at commas. Reader 3 does not pause after 'castle'; and Reader 4 does not pause after 'people' or 'castle'.

Reader 5 seems to have the most pauses; this could be a product of his adopting a 'reading-to-children' style. When reader 3 pauses after 'soon', this could indicate that she is analysing 'after her birth' as a phrase, instead of interpreting 'soon after' as a phrase. When under pressure to perform, readers may pause before words that they find difficult to pronounce.

EXERCISE 3 <u>Question 1</u>

	1	2	3	4	5
princess	R	R	F	R	F
Irene	R	R	R	R	R
there	F	F	F	F	F
birth	R	R	R	F	F
strong	R	R	F	F	R
people	F	F	R	F	F
house	F	F	R	F	F
castle	R	R	R	R	R
farmhouse	F	R	R	R	F

Question 1

(a) prɪnsɛs   (b) maʊntɛnz

(c) ʌpɔ̃   (d) maʊntɛnz

(e) mʌðə   (f) pipʌl   (g) maʊntɛn

Notice that she does not produce a nasal consonant in (c) but pronounces the vowel with **nasalization**. This means that the velum has been lowered as the vowel is made allowing air to flow out of the nose as well as out of the mouth.

On the word (a) a native speaker of English might use a schwa or /ɪ/ on the last syllable. But we need to be careful about this – when this word is positioned before a pause a native English speaker might stress the second syllable. However, in a phrase before a word that has stress on the first syllable, as in 'PRINcess CARoline' the first syllable might be stressed.

Question 2

She pronounces what sounds like an /h/ on all of the words except 'whose'. Here something different is used – there is voicelessness, but there seems to be some slight friction, and lip rounding. This could be indicated by using the symbol [ɸ] or by an [h] with a superscript [w] [hʷ]. In Japanese there is a consonant phoneme which is a voiceless bi-labial fricative. Perhaps she is using this sound here. Note also that the next vowel has tight lip-rounding, so this feature could be influencing her pronunciation.

Question 3

(a) bʌ ʃi wəz sɛnʔ sũ ʔaftə hə bɑː θ

(b) wəz bɪlt ʌpɔ̃

(c) tu bi brɔːt ʌp

Notice again on 'soon' (a) that she does not make a nasal consonant but has nasalization on the vowel. It might seem odd that she deletes the /t/ of 'sent' but produces a word-final /t/ in 'brought' and 'built'. Note however that in these two words the next word begins with a vowel, whereas in the case of 'sent' the next word begins with a consonant /s/. We might speculate that the syllable structure of Japanese does not allow sequences of consonants across words to occur frequently, if at all.

EXERCISE 4 Question 4

(a) lıtʌl
(b) fɑðɛ'
(c) ouvər_ə
(d) fərʌv mauntɛnz an variz
(e) parıs
(f) vɛri
(g) aırin
(h) ðɛaɽ
(i) ʔaftə
(j) ənʌðə

Notice that occasionally this speaker uses r-dropping; she does not produce an /r/ in 'father', 'after', or 'another'. We might expect this to happen on the word 'there' as well, but the /r/ here is very 'strong'. In terms of articulation this is a **retroflex** sound. The tip of the tongue is slightly curled back towards the hard palate. The symbol that is used is [ɽ].

EXERCISE 4 Question 5

(a) prınsɛs	**(b)** greıt	**(c)** kɒntri	**(d)** grɑːnd
(e) bɔːn	**(f)** bɑːθ	**(g)** strɔŋ	**(h)** brɔːt
(i) kɒntri	**(j)** lɑdʒ	**(k)** fɑːmhaus	

Interestingly, we find her use of /r/ resembling again the non-rhotic accent of RP. She does not produce an /r/ after vowels. Perhaps the model of pronunciation she has been taught was a non-rhotic one. There seems to be a pattern in her use of a sound which seems to match English /l/. When there is an 'r' in the spelling and it is positioned between vowels, she will produce what sounds like an /l/ to the English ear. And when an 'l' occurs between vowels, she produces what sounds like an /r/, as in 'full of' [fərʌv].

EXERCISE 5 Question 1

In words with initial 'h' in the spelling she produces it in all words except 'his', 'her' and the second occurrence of 'half'.

EXERCISE 5 Question 2

(a) ız ples wɒzə bıldə+bıldə ʌpʰ
(b) ðə prınsɛsə huz neımə wəzə irinə

(c) bɑ̟ta ʃi wəz sɛn suːn ɑ̟ftər ər bərðeɪ
(d) bikɔzə ər mɑ̟ðər wɒz nɒt^{h} vɛri strɔŋgə

EXERCISE 5 Question 3

This might indicate a syllable structure in Italian where words tend to end in a vowel sound.

EXERCISE 5 Question 4

(a) litɛl
(b) (1st) moʊnteɪnz (2nd) məʊnteɪnz (3rd) maʊnteɪn
(c) bjutifʊl
(d) bikɔzə

EXERCISE 5 Question 5

Yes, she is an 'r-pronouncer'.

EXERCISE 5 Question 6

She does not use weakening in any of these words.

EXERCISE 6 Question 1

On the word 'beautiful' the speaker uses a voiced labio-dental fricative. Perhaps the next sound in the word, a back rounded vowel has led to this.

EXERCISE 6 Question 2

Both 'mother' and 'one' use vowels that English speakers might use, [mʌðər] and [wɒn]. But the other words have a long low back vowel; we could use the symbol [ɒː].

EXERCISE 7

In the case of 'full of mountains' all of the readers make this prominent, as native-speaking readers probably would. In the case of 'one of the mountains' all of the readers make this non-prominent, again, as native speakers probably would. The Italian speaker seems to give equal prominence to both words in 'another mountain', and the Spanish speaker gives slightly more prominence to 'another' than on 'mountain', but perhaps differentiates between them somewhat

less than a native-speaking reader might. The Japanese reader seems to foreground the word 'mountain'.

Note that the native speaker also has equal prominence on 'another mountain'
in her child reading, and more prominence on 'another' in her 'adult' reading.
Placement of prominence is always a matter for the speaker's judgement, not the
product of rules.

Below is a complete suggested transcription for each of the non-native speaking readers. Normal word boundaries have been maintained for ease of reading.

JAPANESE

ðɛː wɒz wãs ə lɪtʌl prɪnsɛs + ɸus faðɛ wʌz kiːŋg + oʊvər‿ə greɪt kɒntri + fər‿ʌv
maʊntɛnz an variz + hɪz parɪs wəz bɪlt ʌpɔ̃ + wʌnəv ðə maʊntɛnz andə wɒz veri
graːnd ən bjutɪfʊɫ + ðə prɪnsɛs + ɸus neɪm wɒz aɪrin + wəz bɔːn ðɛaɽ + bʌ ʃi wəz
sɛnʔ sũ + ʔaftə hə baːθ + bikɔz hə mʌðə wəẓ nɒt veri strɔŋ + tu bi brɔːt ʌp + baɪ
kɒntri pipʌl + ɪnə ladʒ haʊs + haf kasəl haf faːmhaʊs + ɒn ðə saɪd ɒv ənʌðə
maʊntɛn

ITALIAN

ðə prɪnsɛs an ðə gǫblin + ðɛr wɒzə wʌns ə litɛl prɪnsɛsə + hus faðər wʌz kɪŋgə
ovər ə gret kʌntri fʊləv moʊnteɪnz + an valiz ɪz ples wɒzə bɪldə-bɪldə ʌpʰ
wǫn‿əf ðə məʊnteɪnz an wəz veri grænd an bjutifʊl + ðə prɪnsɛsə + huz neɪmə
wəzə irinə + wəz bərn ðer + bǫtə ʃi wəz sɛn suːn ǫftər ər bərðeɪ + bərð bikɔzə ər
mǫðər wɒz nɒtʰ veri strɔŋgə + tu bi brɔːt ʌpʰ baɪ kǫntri pipəl ɪn‿ə lartʃ haʊz̦ə +
haf kastəl af farmhaʊz̦ə + ɒn ðə saɪd ʌf ənǫðər maʊnteɪn

SPANISH

ðər wəz wʌns ə liːtəl prɪnsɪs + huz faðər wəz kin oʊvər ə greɪːt kɒːntri fʊl‿ʌv
maʊːntənz ən vaːlɛz + hɪs paːlɛs + wʌz bɪltʰ əpɒn wɒn‿əv ðə maʊːntənz + ən
wʌz veri graːnd ən vjuːtɪfʊɫ + ðə prɪnsɪs + huz neɪm wɒz irenɛ + wɒz bɔːrn ðer
+ bʌʔ ʃi wʌz sɛnt sũːn + aftər hər bəːrθ + bikɔz hər mʌðər wɒz nɒt veːri strɔŋ
+ tu bi brɔːt + ʌpʰ baɪ kɒːntri pipʌl + in‿ə laːrdʒə haʊs + haf kasəɫ + haf h-
farmhaʊs + ɒn ðə saɪd + ɒv‿ənɒːðər maʊːntɛn

'siracucus and elephant highways'

Preview

In this unit we will be extending and developing our study of the meanings and uses of intonation patterns.

Background

In both of the two recordings that will be used in this unit, the speakers are telling their listener about their experiences – they are telling stories. But none of the speakers has prepared beforehand. So this means they have to decide as they are speaking what events they are going to include, in what order, how they are going to express their reactions and feelings, and how they are going to involve the listener. In other words, these stories are not really monologues even though the listeners hardly say anything at all.

Sequence 1

In this recording a young woman tells of her trip with a friend up the Amazon River in Brazil. They started by flying into Rio de Janeiro.

> . . . and off we went to Rio + and um I I hadn't given it any thought at all and the next thing I knew we went up to + Manaus which is a free port up on the Amazon + where we + met + some chap who'd got a boat um which was rather like the

African Queen* + um and I felt like Katharine Hepburn* + and we then um went
5   in this boat up + the Amazon and then off up one of the tributaries + um where we
then came across this little South American tribe + some Indians um who lent us a
canoe + (yeah) so we then + left most of our luggage behind and just took a ruck-
sack with a couple of tee shirt and a toothbrush and a bag of rice and a rifle + and
then we had a hammock and a + mosquito net which didn't bode well + (hm) and
10 off we went um then on + foot uh it was very wet and uh + we just we and the
vegetation was very thick and we you had we had a guide + and a cook + and
another another boy + and um so we went off in our canoes and uh then left those
+ in the side in the some reeds somewhere and then walked + um we walked for
four days into the jungle + um the mosquitoes were appalling the rain was
15 appalling + um and we were hungry and in four days it was just very interesting
that you could feel yourself reverting back to nature + (any danger did you were
you in any danger at any time) well if yes if when we first got into the + actually
stood out of the canoe and into the jungle + um our guide had eh bare feet + and
he + I mean he didn't speak any any English at all but um + suddenly you could
20 see that he just leapt and you could see the whites of his eyes and he'd trodden +
on + a deadly poisonous snake something called a siracucu and he'd have been
dead in thirty seconds if it had bitten him + um and without him I mean he was our
guide and without him we would never have got out again um so that was + quite
dangerous (mmm) and I mean who knows what sort of + animals was (yeah) or
25 reptiles were around at night spiders or whatever + (did you see other animals I
mean you must have seen monkeys) monkeys yeah and turtles and + but you know
the vegetation was so I mean it was so thick that + I mean you couldn't see + I
don't know ten uh ten feet in front of you + and so we literally had machetes and
were were cutting our way through the through the undergrowth + but the flora and
30 fauna was I mean it was just beautiful + um + you know it was a very it was an
incredible experience really because it's very unusual in your lives that you're + in
the civilisation that we live in uh that you ever go without that you actually are +
concerned for your + for your welfare and that + you wonder where your next
meal's going to come from . . .

* a film made in the 1950s with Humphrey Bogart and Katharine Hepburn in the lead roles. The
film is set during the First World War and centres on a trip down a river in Africa in a dilapidated
boat, called the African Queen.

Exercise 1

Listen to the sequence about the deadly snake (from line 17 'when we first got into . . .' up to line 22 '. . . if it had bitten him . . .').

Question 1

Which tones are used on the following items: (a) bare feet (b) English (c) suddenly (d) leapt (e) whites (f) eyes (g) trodden (h) deadly (i) poisonous (j) snake (k) siracucu (l) dead (m) thirty seconds?

Question 2

Why do you think this choice of tone predominates in this part of her narrative about the Amazon trip?

Exercise 2

At several points in her narrative, she uses falling tones that begin on a high pitch, or with 'high onset' (*see* Unit 4).

Question 1

Listen to the sequence and locate these high falls.

Question 2

In this sequence, the speaker is relating her experiences in the Amazon, and talking about the significance of those experiences. In this context or speaking situation, what meaning could we associate with these high falls? (You might want to think about the use of high falls by the grandmother and her grandson in Unit 4.)

Exercise 3

There are three times when the speaker gives a list in her narrative. A common observation about the intonation of lists in English is that the last item in the list will be said with a falling tone, and all the previous items will be said with a rising tone, or a mid-level tone, or a falling tone that doesn't fall very low in the pitch range. If the list is left incomplete, the speaker will show this by using a rising tone on the last-mentioned item. So, for example, (a) below is a complete list of three flavours of ice cream, but (b) is an **in**complete list – these three are mentioned but there are other unmentioned ones.

(a) we have↗vanilla↗chocolate and↘strawberry
(b) we have↗vanilla↗chocolate↗strawberry . . .

In Questions 1–3 below, you will be asked to identify the tones used on the items in her lists. Then, for each of the lists, consider to what extent you think this speaker follows the intonation pattern for listing described above. Does there seem to be any variation in her use of the pattern, and if so, can you think of any reasons for there to be variation?

Question 1

Listen to the list of the three people who accompanied them on their journey (lines 11 to 12). Does she use the listing pattern as in (a)? (Spaces have been left for you to use directional arrows to represent the direction of pitch movement.)

. . . we had a   guide   and a   cook and another   boy . . .

Question 2

Now listen to the list of the items they took with them in the canoe (lines 7 to 9). Which type of tone is used on the underlined words?

. . . and just took a   <u>rucksack</u> with a couple of   <u>tee shirt</u> and a   <u>toothbrush</u> and a bag of   <u>rice</u> and a   <u>rifle</u> and then we had a   <u>hammock</u> and a +   <u>mosquito net</u> which didn't bode well . . .

Question 3

The third list is slightly different from the previous two; it is a list of things they experienced. Listen to this list (lines 13 to 15) and identify the type of tone she uses on the underlined words.

. . . we walked for four days into the jungle + um the   <u>mosquitoes</u> were <u>appalling</u> the   <u>rain</u> was   <u>appalling</u> + um we were very   <u>hungry</u> . . .

Exercise 4

At the beginning of her narrative the woman is providing various types of information about the early stages of the trip down the Amazon. Some of this information is given in relative clauses following the noun. Some examples are as follows:

(a) Manaus which is a free port up the Amazon
(b) we met some chap who'd got a boat
(c) some Indians um who lent us a canoe

When speakers are giving information, we've seen that they commonly use a falling tone. Listen again to examples (b) and (c). These two examples look identical in their grammatical structure: is the intonation pattern she uses identical?

Exercise 5

Listen to the intonation on the relative clause which follows her list of what they took with them: '. . . and a mosquito net which didn't bode well . . .'. Does she use a falling tone or a rising tone here, and how might you account for this choice?

Exercise 6

Towards the beginning of her narrative, she mentions the film 'The African Queen' and compares their boat with the one in the film. She also compares her feelings of being in a similar situation to the female lead in the film, played by Katharine Hepburn. What tone does she use in these phrases?

Sequence 2

In this recording two young women in their twenties are describing their experiences in Zimbabwe on a volunteer programme in the national parks. The recording was made outside in one of the parks. (At one point you can hear what sounds like a jeep or truck going past.)

A: . . . and then we were living at the next + sort of clump of trees next to the water
pan where you're not allowed to go if you're + not a tourist + if you are a tourist
so it's like there's big signs everywhere I took a picture of one of the signs saying
'Please do not drive off the road' 'cause we that's the first thing we did drove
5 straight off the road straight into the trees and set up our camp and there's actually
elephant prints like an elephant highway right the way through near where our
camp was and we saw these prints next week we sat there we saw all these
elephants (B: that's where we were) just trucking past us well I 'Oh my God'
we're right in the middle of an elephant highway (B: about ten feet away) oh yeah
10 . . . B: it was wonderful 'cause we went on two or three night safaris + we had a
brilliant driver + and um he was sort of like quite adventurous I think he enjoyed
it just as much as we did and we we were sort of like travelling to different water
pans obviously to try to find some lion + um we only actually saw one but that was
amazing (uhuh) wasn't it it was a (A: lioness) lioness and we actually saw her +
15 well she was actually surrounding + a um a herd of elephants who were drinking
at a pan I don't know whether she was actually stalking (mm) or whether she was
actually um just waiting to have a drink but it was amazing . . . [the listener asks if
they had a sense of danger] A: . . . no you feel incredibly safe actually + I think
because I mean the lion appeared quite docile + that's what that's what really
20 struck me is that all the ali- all the animals even the elephants + appear very docile
and they don't they don't charge about or anything like that I think so long as you
sort of like um respect them + and respect their territory and respect their own
space + then they're not actually they're not going to hurt you at all + not at all . . .
[the listener then asked them how the work they were doing in this area compared
25 with the work they had done in other areas] A: . . . it was it was different (B: physical?) um + 'cause the last project that we actually did we were actually construct-
ing a whole new water pan + so we actually had to design it and then + dig + the
space inside and then cement round the outside so that it could be filled with water
and that was quite tough digging digging the ground + having to shovel it all out
30 was quite tough working then obviously mixing the cement (B: cementing we did
cementing that's hard work we know how hard that is) I think I think one of the
um slightly infuriating things is 'cause we only had one truck + um we spent quite
a lot of time waiting around 'cause we had to go and collect rocks + and sand +
from + elsewhere which would often be sort of like a two or three hour truck jour-
35 ney away which obviously slows the process down and you just feel + hav-
specially having been somewhere like Gatsi (?) where it was like + non-stop work
work from half five + you know round the clock often you felt you were sitting
there not really doing much + but I think at the end of the day when you actually
see the final product + you realise that . . .

Exercise I

As you listen to the recording, read along with the transcript and note the basic shape of the intonation pattern (high or low rising/falling) used on the following phrases (listed in order of their occurrence).

(a) next to the water pan
(b) and set up our camp
(c) like an elephant highway
(d) near where our camp was
(e) we saw all these elephants
(f) we went on two or three night safaris
(g) we had a brilliant driver
(h) to try to find some lion
(i) who were drinking at a pan
(j) the lion appeared quite docile
(k) they're not going to hurt you at all
(l) and that was quite tough
(m) we spent quite a lot of time waiting around
(n) and collect rocks and sand from elsewhere
(o) which would often be sort of like a two or three hour truck journey away
(p) non-stop work from half five
(q) often you felt you were sitting there not actually doing much

Looking back

We have used this unit to consolidate particular ideas about the role of intonation and the meanings that speakers convey through choice of tone. These storytelling sequences illustrate that intonation is linked to the complex task of organizing the information content of a story, while at the same time taking account of your listener and their task of understanding what you are saying, as well as showing how you recognize the contribution they make by being in the role of listener.

Tasks for discussion or extension

Create the script of the first speaker's narrative about her return journey back to Rio. Include points that she mentions in Sequence 1, for example: ' . . . and then we returned the canoe and caught another boat . . .'. Then read your script aloud, and consider what use of rising and falling tones you might make.

Ask someone you know to tell you about a holiday or travel experiences. Make a recording and analyse their use of intonation, paying attention to their use of intonation in any lists or when informing the listener of events or relying on the listener's knowledge or similar experiences.

Unit 11 Key and comments

EXERCISE 1 Question 1 and 2

She uses falling tones on all of the items. In this part of the narrative about her experiences, she is giving new information to her listener. He has asked her about any dangerous episodes, but she knows he has no particular expectations or foreknowledge about what happened to her.

EXERCISE 2 Question 1 and 2

She uses high falls on (1) 'yes' at line 17, (2) 'see' at line 20, (3) 'without' at line 22, and again on 'without' at line 32. She seems to be emphasizing these particular items, that is, telling her listener to pay special attention to them. If falling tones are usually associated with stating or asserting, these high falls seem to be associated with strong statements. In (1) we might paraphrase her meaning as 'yes, indeed' or 'yes, I most certainly was'. In (2) she seems to modify the idiom 'you could see the whites of his/her/their eyes' (meaning that someone is extremely close to you) to something like 'you really could *literally* see the whites of his eyes, because his eyes were wide open in horror'. In (3) the word 'without' is brought into special focus because of the contrast with 'with him', emphasizing how essential their guide was to their survival – being with him means safety, being without him means disaster. In (4) there is again a contrast involved, this time with the normal state of having all you need to survive, or not having these basic requirements.

EXERCISE 3 Question 1

On this complete list of three, she uses a rising tone on the first item ('guide') and a falling tone on 'cook' but this does not finish at a low point, so both these tone choices are signalling that the list is not complete. The third item, 'boy' has a lower fall. But this last falling tone does not fall to the lowest part of her pitch range; if it did this would seem to show the end of her story and it is obvious that she is going to say much more – 'the story continues'.

EXERCISE 3 Question 2

All of the items have falling tones (although not low falls) except 'rifle' and 'mosquito net', which have rising tones. There does not seem to be much pitch movement on 'bag of rice' so we might label this a mid-level tone. The rising tone on 'mosquito net' is a low rise, but the rising tone on 'rifle' is interesting because it is a very high rise. We might ask ourselves the question: why has she decided to use such a high rise on this particular item? One possibility is that she is drawing attention to this point of information, but then since it is new information for her listener, one might expect a falling tone. Another possibility is that she is trying to engage her listener at this point – to say something like 'I am sure you realize the significance of the fact that we had a rifle, that is, this was no ordinary tourist outing, but one fraught with danger.' One indication that her listener has got this message is that he says 'yeah'. Perhaps he does this to show her that he has recognized her reason for highlighting the word 'rifle'.

EXERCISE 3 Question 3

She uses a high-rising tone on 'hungry'. This could show that this is a partial list of the (unpleasant) experiences they were having, and that there were others that she hasn't mentioned, for example, 'sleeping in the hammocks was terrible'. But again, she could also be expressing something like the following: I'm sure this information is no surprise to you – of course we were hungry – we could only carry very little food with us on foot. Here again she could be engaging her listener, making his understanding and expectations contribute to her narrative.

EXERCISE 4

On (b) she uses a falling pattern, but on (c) she uses a rising pattern. This difference seems difficult to explain in terms of the grammatical structure, which is identical, and the fact that in both cases she is giving information to her listener, and one would therefore expect falling tones on both. We can perhaps apply the interpretation used above in Exercise 3: when she tells her listener about getting a canoe she has just said that they were going up a tributary of the Amazon. Perhaps she is again relying on his understanding that canoes are necessary on narrow waterways, and uses rising intonation to say something like 'are you with me – do you understand what I've just said about the canoe?'

EXERCISE 5

Again, it is possible that the rising pitch on '... bode well' shows that she is sending a message something like: 'I'm sure you understand what I mean' using this intonation pattern.

EXERCISE 6

She uses low-rising tone on both 'African Queen' and 'Katharine Hepburn'. This seems to show that she **expects** her listener to be familiar with this film and to recognize and understand what she is alluding to. She doesn't need to inform him about the film and its character – this is knowledge that they both share already.

EXERCISE I

All of the clauses in the list could be described as 'declarative clauses' that is, clauses, which by their structure and position in the narrative, seem to be giving information to the listener. The speakers use falling tones on the following: (a), (b), (e), (g), (i), (k), (l), (p) and (n). They use high-rising tones on the following clauses: (c), (d), (f), (h), (j), (m), (o) and (q).

It seems impossible to predict which of the clauses in the list will have high rises and which will have falls. But we can speculate that at particular points in their description of their experiences the two storytellers turn their attention to their listener. They seem to be saying to their listener, 'are you following?' and to be building understanding with the listener. We could use the term 'building solidarity' to describe this process. We could also link this use of rising tones with the idea of 'orientation to the addressee' that has been associated with rising tones used, for example, in asking questions (*see* Unit 4). This use of high-rising tones at points where the speaker seems to be giving information, but also seems to be seeking some sort of involvement with the listener, has been called 'high-rising terminals' or 'upspeak'.

Some contemporary novelists seem to have recognized the use of 'upspeak'.

For example, in Ian McEwan's novel *Enduring Love*, the narrator says the following of the character called 'Parry': 'He had his generation's habit of making a statement on the rising inflection of a question' (1998: 24). This is shown when the character speaks by the use of a question mark. Here is an example from p. 66: 'It's very simple?' In Iain Banks' 1992 novel *The Crow Road*, a particular character's dialogue is treated in the same way. Here is an example: 'I was in Frankfurt,' she said. 'Seeing this friend from college?' (p. 78).

'marmalade sandwiches'

Preview

In this unit we will examine a wide range of features that occur in a conversation between an adult and a child. The child's pronunciation is developing, and several of the forms he uses do not 'match' an adult's usage. Because his system is evolving, it will sometimes be a challenge to decide what category of sound is being produced. The adjustments in pronunciation that the adult makes will also be considered.

Background

The child in this sequence is male, aged three years six months. He and his parents are visiting his aunt and uncle. The recording was made in the morning in the sitting room of the house. The child was playing with a manual typewriter and old envelopes and stickers. His aunt has set up a small cassette recorder in order to make a recording of her nephew. The child is familiar with cassette recorders used in playback mode only; he has his own and enjoys playing special song and story tapes on it. The sequence begins just as he has noticed that the tape recorder is on. When his aunt comes into the room, she pretends that the tape is rewinding not recording in order to get her recording.

The child's parents both have Scottish accents, as do his two older brothers. They live in a small town in eastern Scotland.

Exercise 1

Listen to the recording and answer the following questions on the child's vowels and consonants.

(Transcribing conversations with a child of this age is very difficult. The adults may not be certain what exactly the child is trying to say or intends to say, but instead of saying 'sorry' or 'what' each time, they will make a guess based on the context, and, at times may even respond with an 'all-purpose' or ambiguous comment. For example, at line 21 it seems that the child's aunt isn't sure whether he has said 'really' or 'ready,' so she makes two responses – one for each option.)

'C' stands for the child, 'M' his mother, and 'A' his aunt.

	C:	oh is th- this one is going have a tune on this radio is going to have a tune on it
	M:	[barely audible] you going to sing a tune for it
	C:	but it doesn't need a tune for it [A comes into the room]
5	**C:**	is that needing to be going down [referring to the recorder]
	A:	no it's OK
	C:	does it . . .
	A:	it's not finished yet
	C:	hasn't it why hasn't it finished yet
10	**A:**	it still has a way to go yet
	C:	and how do you pop it do . . . how do you pop those ones down
	A:	it's very very difficult I'll show you later
	C:	how do you make that bit open
	A:	that's another button that's underneath
15	**C:**	em th- one of these buttons
	A:	that's not buttons that's where the sound comes when it's ready but it's not ready yet
	C:	comes out of those little holes
	A:	they look like little holes don't they
20	**C:**	but they aren't really [ready]
	A:	no they're not really it's not ready yet
	C:	why is it not ready yet why is it all quiet
	A:	cause it's a very slow one this one
	C:	just a very slow one
25	**A:**	yeah it's a very slow one [clicks as A checks recorder]
	C:	why are you doing something about that
	A:	I'm just checking it
	C:	did you leave it too long
	A:	I'm not sure I think it's OK

30 **C:** (unintell) do these buttons pop up theirself do they

    A: yep (C: they pop . . .) when it's finished

    C: they pop up theirself

    A: yep they do

    C: (unintell) it a very slow one that one

35 **A:** sorry

    C: why is it a very slow one

    A: I don't know + maybe it's not a very good one

    C: I'm putting this way (unintell) go faster   I maked it go faster

    A: you made it go faster

40 **C:** yeah by turning it that way

    A: ah ha   that's very clever

    C: to make the tape go down a wee bit

    A: oh right + oh that was a good thought

    C: ma- ma- marmalade sandwiches + he said   Teddy said marmalade

45   sandwiches

    A: [laughing] marmalade sandwiches   are they good marmalade sand-
        wiches

    C: yeah but I don't like marmalade sandwiches

    A: you don't

50 **C:** but Paddington bear does

    A: Paddington bear does   are they his favourite

    C: yes + marmalade + he's from darkest Peru

    A: is he   very far away

    C: he's his + very far away [child pressing typewriter keys]

55 **C:** why does these ones fly?

    A: what

    C: why does those ones fly

    A: don't know [child is playing with the typewriter] . . .

    A: are you finished typing

60 **C:** I'm trying to get it in the middle again

    A: oh . . . [child is singing softly] . . .

    C: it needs to go this way up

    A: does it need to go that way up

    C: right + now + what are they + how do you pop these ones up

65 **A:** they go by themselves

    C: why do they

    A: cause they're automatic

C: how does it go that way   round and round again and again
A: yep   that's the way it goes   it winds around and round
70 **C:** winds around and round and round why does it not loosen this
    one
A: that's the way it's made
C: why is it the way it's made   what does that one do
A: that one is eject + it ejects it + that makes the tape go out
75   . . .

Question 1

How does the child produce the consonant clusters in the following words. (Line references precede each word.)

(a)	1	tune
(b)	4	doesn't need
(c)	9	hasn't it
(d)	9	finished
(e)	11	ones
(f)	18	holes
(g)	20	aren't
(h)	22	quiet
(i)	24	slow
(j)	32	theirself
(k)	38	faster
(l)	48	don't
(m)	55	fly
(n)	73	it's

Question 2

Speakers of English have two possible pronunciations of the nasal consonant in various word forms with '-ing-'. For example, in continuous verb forms such as 'I'm tak**ing** this away' and 'He's go**ing** soon' speakers might use a velar nasal (/teɪkɪŋ/ /goʊɪŋ/) or an alveolar nasal (/teɪkɪn/ /goʊɪn/).

The patterns of the use of velar or alveolar nasal for '-ing' seem to be related to stylistic factors or sociolinguistic meanings in English speech. For example, in careful, rehearsed speech, a speaker may use the velar nasal, but in spontaneous, highly colloquial and informal speech the alveolar nasal may be used. Some sociolinguistic studies have identified /- n/ versus /-ŋ/ as being involved in marking 'vernacular' speech as opposed to prestigious pronunciation in contemporary English. In early twentieth century England /n/ seems to have been an upper-class pronunciation feature. One type of evidence we have for this is the representation of speech in novels. For example, in Arthur Conan Doyle's *The Lost World* (1912) the speech of an upper-class character, Lord John Roxton, shows him to be a user of /-n/ as in: 'Don't mind tak**in'** a risk, do you?', whereas a middle class Irishman, Edward Malone, is not shown as a user of /n/ in words with '-ing' (p. 50). Contemporary sociolinguistic studies have also found it to be associated with colloquial speech. See, for example, Trudgill (1974).

Which of these two nasal consonants does the child use in the following words. (Line references precede each word.)

(a) 5 needi<u>ng</u> to be goi<u>ng</u> down
(b) 26 doi<u>ng</u> someth<u>ing</u>
(c) 38 putting this way
(d) 40 turning it
(e) 50 Paddington bear
(f) 60 I'm trying to get it

Which of the two nasal consonants does the child's aunt use in:

(a) 27 just checking it
(b) 51 Paddington bear does
(c) 59 are you finished typing

In words such as 'rotten' or 'mutton', where the spelling would seem to indicate that the pronunciation will be an alveolar plosive followed by an unstressed vowel and then an alveolar nasal, speakers often move directly from the plosive to the nasal without releasing the plosive with a puff of air. This means that the nasal is 'exploded' rather than the plosive, and there is no vowel in the second syllable. As the closure for the plosive is being made, the velum is lowered, so that the puff of air is released through the nose and not through the mouth. The process is known as **nasal plosion**. Because the nasal consonant is the nucleus of the second syllable, it is called a **syllabic nasal**. This is symbolized by [n̩].

Question 3

In the sequence there are three occurrences of the word 'button'. Two are pronounced by the adult and one by the child. How are each of these three produced – with nasal plosion or with a sequence consonant–vowel–nasal?

(a) 14 another button
(b) 15 one of these buttons
(c) 16 that's not buttons

In words such as 'bottle' or 'riddle' where again it would seem from the spelling that the pronunciation would be an alveolar plosive followed by an unstressed vowel and then an /l/, speakers usually move directly from the plosive to a position for the /l/. While the closure for the alveolar plosive is being made, the sides of the tongue are lowered and the air is released laterally – across the sides of the tongue. This process is called **lateral plosion**. The /l/ becomes the nucleus of the second syllable as there is no vowel sound as its nucleus. The symbol used is [l̩]. It is referred to as a 'syllabic-l'.

Question 4

There are three occurrences of words with a /t/ or /d/ with an /l/ following. One is 'little', produced by the child at line 18 followed in the next utterance by the adult saying the same word. Then at line 60 the child says 'middle'. Transcribe these words, showing whether lateral plosion is used or not.

(a) 18 those little holes
(b) 19 like little holes
(c) 60 in the middle again

Question 5

Listen to the following words; what sound do you hear in the child's speech for the consonant underlined in the orthographic forms?

(a)   1 radio
(b)   9 yet
(c) 11 you
(d) 20 really? ready?
(e) 22 ready yet
(f) 24 very slow
(g) 26 why are you
(h) 30 theirself
(i) 38 faster
(j) 40 turning
(k) 44 marmalade (also 48/52)
(l) 50 bear

(m) 52 da<u>r</u>kest

(n) 54 fa<u>r</u> away

(o) 55 f<u>l</u>y (also 57)

(p) 62 <u>w</u>ay

(q) 70 a<u>r</u>ound and <u>r</u>ound and <u>r</u>ound

Question 6

Briefly describe the child's system with regards to /l/ and /r/ in initial or medial position in words. In the cases where /l/ is part of a consonant cluster, how does the child pronounce these sounds? What sound(s) does he use for the glide /j/ as in in 'you' or 'yet'?

Question 7

The child's mother has a non-rhotic accent and his father's accent is rhotic. Judging from the data here, does the child's speech show rhoticity or non-rhoticity or a mixture?

Question 8

One characteristic of the Scottish accent is that the vowels in words such as 'take', 'break', 'tape', and so on are monophthongs /e:/. Other varieties of English have vowels that are diphthongal in quality, e.g. /eɪ/. The same is true of the back half-close vowel as in 'soap', 'coat', 'rope'; many Scottish speakers of English will use /o:/, whereas other varieties will have /ou/ or /oʊ/. Compare the vowels produced by the child and by his aunt in the following words – which are monophthongs and which are diphthongs?

Aunt	Child
12 later	13 make
19 holes	18 holes
23 slow	24 slow
33 they	32 they
39 made	38 maked
69 goes	40 way
72 made	42 make
	66 they
	68 go
	73 made

Exercise 2

Answer the following questions on the child's use of intonation.

Question 1

The child seems to have a intonation pattern that he uses very frequently. Listen to the following utterances. What do you consider to be the features of this pattern or tune in terms of direction of the pitch movement, the pitch of the first syllable and the pitch of the last syllable?

(a)   5 is that needing to be going down
(b)   9 why hasn't it finished yet
(c) 11 how do you pop those ones down
(d) 13 how do you make that bit open
(e) 22 why is it not ready yet why is it all quiet
(f) 26 why are you doing something about that
(g) 36 why is it a very slow one
(h) 38 I maked it go faster
(i) 40 by turning it that way
(j) 42 to make the tape go down a wee bit
(k) 55 why do those ones fly (also 57)

Question 2

The child uses different patterns on the following utterances: how would you describe these? Use curving lines on a stave or arrows to represent the pitch movement.

(a) 15 one of these buttons
(b) 18 comes out of those little holes
(c) 20 but they aren't really
(d) 28 did you leave it too long
(e) 30 these buttons pop up theirself do they
(f) 32 they pop up theirself
(g) 50 but Paddington bear does
(h) 60 I'm trying to get it in the middle again

Question 3

There are three instances where a pattern is used on a single syllable. Draw a representation of the pattern you hear:

―――――――

―――――――

1 oh

―――――――

―――――――

64 right

―――――――

―――――――

64 now

🔍 Question 4

At one point the child goes into the kitchen, and from there calls to his uncle. This extract is at the end of the conversation. Listen to his intonation and transcribe the pattern you hear:

―――――――

―――――――

uncle david

🔍 Question 5

Describe the use of paralinguistic features at line 44 when the child says 'marmalade sandwiches'. What do you think the child is trying to convey with these features?

🔍 Question 6

After his aunt comments 'oh that was a good thought' (line 43), the child introduces the topic of marmalade sandwiches and of bears (his own teddy bear and Paddington bear) and their love for marmalade sandwiches. His aunt picks up on this topic and questions him about it. Once a topic has been introduced by a speaker in a conversation, the speakers thereafter use a low or low-rising intonation pattern or alternatively general low-pitch range when referring to the topic to signal its status in the conversation as 'given', unless there is some reason to mark it otherwise, e.g. if the speaker feels the topic is 'cold' and needs to be reintroduced. The adult use a low slightly rising pattern when she says: 'are they good marmalade sandwiches?' Does the child do the same when he says: 'but I don't like marmalade sandwiches'?

Looking back

In this unit we have seen some indication of the complexity of the process of learning the pronunciation of your first language. Perhaps it is appropriate that this is covered in the last unit of this workbook, because it highlights the stages through which the complex rules of pronunciation are acquired, a period of learning that people never have any recollection of. We have also seen that children as young as three and a half years are able to control and manipulate the features of pitch movement, and prominence and non-prominence. Perhaps this in itself is an indication of how central these features are. The way this child's system of liquids and glides is developing also serves as a reminder that these sounds share many features, e.g. voicing, lack of friction, and are very similar to vowels, both in articulatory terms, and in the case of /l/ and /n/, in the function it can perform in the syllable.

Tasks for extension and discussion

Make a recording of a young child speaking, and analyse his or her pronunciation. Children develop their sound systems at a remarkable rate, so it would be interesting to make a series of recordings over time and compare them.

Make a recording which includes an adult, and examine how that adult makes changes in pronunciation when speaking with the child. Consider what this may show about people's pronunciation repertoire.

Do you know of words or forms of words (in English or any other language) that are stereotypical forms used by young children, or by adults when speaking to them? When these are analysed in terms of sounds and syllable structure, what patterns do you find?

Unit 12 Key and comments

EXERCISE 1 **Question 1**

	Line	Child form	Comment
(a)	1	tju:n	same as adult
(b)	4	dʌznʔni:d	[ʔ] for [t]
(c)	9	hæzntɪt	same as adult
(d)	9	sɪnɪst	[ʃt] as [st-] and [f] as [s]
(e)	11	wɒns	voiceless [s] or [z]?
(f)	18	hols	c uses [s] for [z]
(g)	20	ɑ:rnt	same as adult
(h)	22	ksaɪət	substitutes [ks] for [kw]
(i)	23	slo:	monophthong
(j)	32	-sɛlʷf	[l] with features of [w]?
(k)	38	fæstɛ:	same as adult
(l)	48	dɔ:nʔ	[ʔ] for [t]
(m)	55	fwaɪ	substitutes [fw] for [fl]
(n)	73	ɪs	[t] not present

GENERAL COMMENTS

The child is using glottal stops in (b) and (l); this is a common feature of Scottish English accents. Notice that in (m) the child seems to 'prefer' to have two consonants in a cluster articulated in the same position – both [f] and [w] are labial, whereas [l] is alveolar. The pronunciation of 'finished' is interesting in this respect. Note that all the child's consonants in his pronunciation of this word are alveolar, whereas the adult form would have three different places of articulation. Even though we could say he is making 'substitutions', note that he keeps the voicing the same. When consonants in a word all share the same place of articulation they are called **homorganic**.

His pronunciation of the word 'theirself' is interesting from the point of viewing of maximizing similarity between consonant articulations. The [l] does not sound like an alveolar liquid, but sounds perhaps more vowel-like, with rounding (hence the choice of [w]. Perhaps there is also some velarization here, i.e. like that for 'dark -l'. The voicing in the final consonant of (e) 'ones' seems very weak. Perhaps there is voicing to begin with, but it dies out quickly.

His pronunciation of 'quiet' is fascinating – why should [s] be used here? It is a pity we don't have him using more words with /kw-/, such as 'quick' to provide more evidence.

Question 2

(a) [n] in needing to; [ŋ] in going
(b) doing [ŋ] something [ŋ]
(c) putting [n]
(d) turning it [n]
(e) Paddington bear [n]
(f) trying to [ŋ]

Notice that the child sometimes uses the [n] in one of the typical environments that adult speakers often use it – before [t] in the next word (needing to, trying to). He may have this as a general rule of pronunciation, because he does the same in 'Paddington bear'.

Question 2 (adult)

(a) checking it [n]
(b) Paddington [ŋ]
(c) typing [ŋ]

Question 3

(a) (adult) bʌtn̩ has nasal plosion
(b) (child) bʌtʰənz does not
(c) (adult) bʌtʰənz no nasal plosion

Note that the adult uses nasal plosion when she uses the word for the first time, but after her nephew has said it, she uses the same pronunciation as he does. Perhaps she is following his way of pronouncing this word. Note also how strong the aspiration is here from both of them. Children learning English seem to have to sort out how to use aspiration, sometimes they use too little and sometimes too much. The aspiration that this child uses on words like 'pop up' is also very strong. (See PE5 p. 144.)

Question 4

(a) (child) lɪtəl – no lateral plosion
(b) (adult) lɪtəl – no lateral plosion
(c) (child) mɪdʊlʷ – no lateral plosion

Notice again how the adult seems to follow the child's pronunciation. Lateral plosion is normal in her pronunciation.

Question 5

(a) radio [r]
(b) yet [j]
(c) (twice) you [j] both times
(d) really [lɛdi] or ready [lɛdi]
(e) ready [lɛdi] yet [lɛt]
(f) very slow [vɛdislo] just [dzʌst]
(g) [waɪɑːju]
(h) theirself [ðɛːsɛlʷf]
(i) (twice) faster [fastɛː]
(j) turning [tɛːnɪn]
(k) marmalade (all three times) [mɑːmɑːleɪd]
(l) bear [bɛː]
(m) darkest [dɑːkɛst]
(n) far away [fɑləwei] for [l] the tongue tip may be curled back towards the hard palate (a retroflex articulation)
(o) fly [fwaɪ]
(p) way [weː]
(q) round (three times) [waʊnd]

Question 6

In initial position the child seems to show variation between 'r' as an [l]-like sound or an [r]-like sound, but in the word 'round' where the [r] is followed by a back vowel, he uses a [w] which is a labio-velar glide with lip-rounding, i.e. he uses a sound that has a feature of 'backness' (velar). In medial position the target sound 'l' is often a voiced alveolar plosive [d]. In the two examples where /l/ is in a consonant cluster, 'slow' matches an adult's pronunciation but in 'fly' the child uses a sound that has the feature 'labial' – perhaps to match the /f/ which also is labial. Note that in 'slow' the /s/ and /l/ are both alveolar, so these already match in terms of place of articulation. (This is referred to as a **homorganic** cluster.) Initial /j/ is occasionally [l]-like but more consistently a [j].

This child is clearly doing a lot of 'work' to sort out the liquids and glides of the English sound system. His evolving system perhaps reveals how similar these categories of sounds are to each other in English. Perhaps he is hearing their vowel-like or 'melodic' quality, and focusing on that. It would be interesting to know what his earliest usage was. Did he have one category of sound for liquids and glides at one point in his development? Did that category then split into two? It would be interesting to see what happens next in his phonological development.

EXERCISE 1 Question 7

The data shows clear evidence of a non-rhotic pronunciation. In 'far away' where non-rhotic speakers would typically use 'linking-r' he inserts an [l]-like sound.

EXERCISE 1 Question 8

The child's aunt uses diphthongs with the one exception of line 72 'made'. The child consistently uses monophthongs.

EXERCISE 2 Question 1

The pattern could be represented as

The key features are mid onset with a falling pattern followed by a rise-fall which is extended over the last few syllables which have long vowels. The final pitch movement is a fall to mid in the pitch range.

EXERCISE 2 Question 2

(a) one of these buttons

(b) comes out of those little holes

(c) but they aren't really

(d) did you leave it too long

(e) these buttons pop up theirself do they

(f) they pop up theirself

(g) but Paddington bear does

(h) I'm trying to get it in the middle again

On the tag question the child uses a rising pattern. On all the others he uses a falling tone, but without the rising movement or 'stretched' pitch movement in the examples in Question 1.

GENERAL COMMENTS ON THESE INTONATION PATTERNS
The child seems to have one pattern (that in Question 1) that he uses on questions and when he is telling his aunt about what he has done and why. He uses a pattern with a sharper falling pitch movement on utterances which confirm or follow on from something his aunt has said, e.g. 'one of these buttons', 'but they aren't ready yet', or 'they pop up theirselves'. This is also used when he is speculating about something: 'one of these buttons' and 'did you leave it too long'. In trying to account for his use of these varied patterns, we might hypothesize that his extended rise-fall is for raising a topic, and he uses a sharper falling contour when he is responding or continuing a topic.

EXERCISE 2 <u>Question 3</u>

(a) oh

(b) right   **(c)** now

The pattern on 'oh' might convey 'something new and unexpected'; 'right' and 'now' seem to match the fall from mid to low which would be used by adults when these words are functioning as 'transition markers' – words that are used to signal that there is a new topic, or a new activity going on. For example, teachers often say to their classes, 'Right, today we're going to work on . . .' or 'Now, you have all worked very hard so let's have a break'.

EXERCISE 2   **Question 4**

uncle david

This is a typical 'calling pattern' in English.

EXERCISE 2   **Question 5**

On this phrase there is overall high pitch, the contour is gradually falling and the voice quality is falsetto. Is the child rendering his teddy's imaginary voice? Is he making his teddy bear a participant in the interaction with his aunt?

EXERCISE 2   **Question 6**

Yes, when he says '. . . marmalade sandwiches', this phrase is very low in his pitch range.

Glossary

The purpose of this glossary is to provide quick reminders for terms that are used in the units, rather than full definitions. Within the entries, capitals are used to show cross-references to other entries. The page numbers after each key word indicate where the term is introduced, defined or discussed.

affricate (9, 102, 103, 133) A plosive consonant that is released not quickly but slowly with audible friction being produced.

affrication (102, 103) When a PLOSIVE is pronounced with a FRICATIVE-type release instead of a quick release, we say that the plosive has affrication.

allophone (138) Different phonetic realizations of a phoneme that are non-distinctive. For example, English /n/ is usually ALVEOLAR but before the DENTAL FRICATIVE in 'tenth' it is dental. However, there are no words in English that are distinguished by a dental NASAL and an alveolar nasal.

alveolar (12) The term for either of the bony ridges that contain the teeth, especially the ridge behind the upper front teeth; any sound made when the tongue touches or comes close to this ridge.

articulators (1) In producing speech the lungs, larynx, lips, tongue, VELUM, etc. work together. The organs of speech are referred to as the articulators, and a distinction is made between those organs of speech which move, the 'active articulators', such as the lips or tongue, and those involved in sound production which do not move, for example, the roof of the mouth or teeth, known as the 'passive articulators'.

aspiration (5, 13–14, 130, 170) The puff of air from the lungs which can follow the release of a PLOSIVE.

assimilation (9, 131, 144, 169) The process by which a sound is influenced by (usually) a following sound so that it becomes more similar to it in VOICING, PLACE OF ARTICULATION, etc.

bi-labial (3, 12) The term for a sound made with both lips.

clear l (27) When the /l/ PHONEME is pronounced without the back of the tongue being pulled back in the region of the VELUM, but with contact between the tip of the tongue at the alveolar ridge, this type of sound is referred to as 'clear l'.

coda (23, 26) CONSONANTS typically occur at the margins of a SYLLABLE. The consonants that occur after the NUCLEUS are said to be positioned in the coda.

complex word (75) A word consisting of a base or root, and one or more other elements. For example, both 'darkness' and 'darken' have the base 'dark', plus the endings used to make a noun or a verb, respectively.

compound word (76–7, 86) A word made up of two or more other words, e.g. 'teapot' from 'tea' and 'pot'.

consonant (1, 123) In phonetics, consonants are described in terms of three features: whether or not there is vibration in the larynx (VOICE); which of the vocal organs are used to make the sound (PLACE OF ARTICULATION); and how the sound is made (MANNER OF ARTICULATION). In terms of the sound system of a particular language, a consonant is a sound that typically occurs at the beginning or end of a syllable, in contrast to a VOWEL which occurs in the centre. It is useful to know that the word derives from Latin *consonans* meaning 'sounding together', that is, with a vowel.

consonant cluster (23–4, 72, 111, 131, 169) A sequence of two or more CONSONANTS within one syllable. For example, the word 'splits' begins with the cluster [spl-] and ends with the cluster [-ts].

dark l (27) When the /l/ PHONEME is pronounced with the back of the tongue hunched up near the VELUM. This is also referred to as velarized l.

dental (8) A sound made with the tip of the tongue positioned in the area of the upper front teeth.

diphthong (21, 165) A VOWEL sound which has a change of quality during a single syllable, as in English [aɪ] in 'rice'.

foot (52, 54) The traditional unit in the analysis of rhythm, made up of strong and weak SYLLABLES in a particular combination, for example, weak–strong (termed an *iamb*) or strong–weak–weak (termed a *dactyl*).

fricative (6) A sound made by bringing the ARTICULATORS (tongue, lips, etc.) so close together that noise ('friction') is made as the air passes through the gap.

glide (10, 24, 114, 116, 168, 171) Glides are produced with no obstruction in the vocal tract, and with not enough narrowing to produce audible friction. So in terms of their features of articulation, they are made like VOWELS. But they behave like CONSONANTS, in that they do not form the NUCLEUS of a SYLLABLE, but occur on the edges of syllables.

glottal stop (xv, 90, 106, 169) A sound made by bringing the vocal cords together, blocking off the air from the lungs, then opening them suddenly.

hard palate (8) An anatomical term for the roof of the mouth behind the ALVEOLAR RIDGE.

homorganic (169, 171) Sounds which are made at the same PLACE OF ARTICULATION. For example, the word 'send' ends with a CONSONANT CLUSTER [-nd] both of which are ALVEOLAR.

intonation (38, 40–41, 43–5, 48, 96–7, 99, 105, 117, 118, 150–51, 155–8, 167, 173–4) The use of changes in the pitch of the voice to convey various types of meaning in speech.

labio-dental (7, 10) A sound made when the lower lip is raised towards or touches the upper front teeth.

lateral plosion (164) The release of a PLOSIVE by lowering the sides of the tongue, as in the word 'bottle'.

linking-r (115–16) In some accents of English /r/ is pronounced between a word ending in a vowel and a following vowel, e.g. the Far East is pronounced as [ðə fɑːr ist] not [ðə fɑː ist].

liquid (10, 138, 168, 171) This type of sound is made with voicing and unhindered air flow. The sounds /l/ and /r/ are examples.

manner of articulation (2) This refers mainly to the type of obstruction or narrowing at the PLACE OF ARTICULATION of a speech sound; for example, if the air from the lungs is blocked completely, this manner of articulation is called a PLOSIVE, but if there is narrowing so that a sound resembling friction is produced, the manner of articulation is called FRICATIVE.

monophthong (21, 165) A VOWEL in which there is no appreciable change in quality, brought about by movement of the ARTICULATORS, during a single syllable.

nasal (2, 162–3) When a nasal sound is made the VELUM is lowered so that air can pass out through the nasal cavity.

nasalisation (144) Lowering of the VELUM during the production of a sound in which air is flowing out through the mouth, allowing air to also flow out through the nose.

nasal plosion (163) The release of a plosive by lowering the VELUM so that air from the lungs can escape through the nose.

non-rhotic (145) Describes an accent where /r/ is pronounced in SYLLABLE-initial position ('run'); between vowels ('sorrow' 'surreal'); but not after vowels, either before a consonant ('apart') or at the end of a word ('fur').

nucleus (23, 26) In the analysis of syllabic structure, the VOWEL is considered to be the core, or essential part of the SYLLABLE. So it is called the nucleus.

onset (23, 26) CONSONANTS occur at the margins of SYLLABLES. A consonant that occurs before the vowel in the syllable is said to be in the onset position.

palatal (11) A speech sound made with the front of the tongue (the middle area) in contact with or near the HARD PALATE.

palato-alveolar (8) A speech sound made with part of the tongue (usually the tip) in the region of the ALVEOLAR ridge, and the middle of the tongue bunched up near the HARD PALATE.

paralinguistic features (141, 142, 174) The prefix 'para-' is derived from the greek preposition meaning 'beside' or 'alongside', so these are features which convey meaning but are not part of the linguistic system. Some examples are relative volume, speed of speech, voice quality, elongation of sounds, etc.

phonemes (xvi, 27) The distinctive sounds of a particular language. If two sounds have the status of phonemes in a language, then this means they are used to distinguish words in that language. For example, in English /t/ and /d/ distinguish the words 'tip' and 'dip' so they are two of the phonemes of English. But if the word 'fill' is pronounced with a CLEAR L or a DARK L, it is still the same word. Although articulated in different ways, these two sounds are just variants of the same phoneme or ALLOPHONES. But in Russian, there are two similar [l] sounds that <u>do</u> distinguish words: the word *ugol* pronounced with a clear l means 'corner', but *ugol'* pronounced with the tongue pulled back means 'coal'.

pitch (38, 40–41, 43, 51, 96, 99, 104) A term used in phonetics for the level of the voice as determined by the vibration of the VOCAL CORDS.

place of articulation (3) Sounds are made by moving the lips, tongue, and lower jaw, etc. to change the size and shape of the channel through which air from the lungs passes. The point of contact or maximum narrowing is referred to as the place of articulation.

plosive (3, 6) A consonant that involves making some sort of closure or tight seal in the vocal tract to block the free passage of air from the lungs, and then releasing this closure quickly, producing a burst of air. (Another term used for this type of sound is a **stop**.)

RP (101, 118, 145) A social rather than a regional accent of English, deemed to be the prestige accent of British English. RP stands for Received Pronunciation.

retroflex (145) An articulation involving the tip of the tongue and the back part of the ALVEOLAR RIDGE or the HARD PALATE.

rhotic (101) An accent of English when /r/ is pronounced whenever it occurs in the spelling. (The terms **r-full** and **r-pronouncing** are also used.)

rhyme (24, 26) In the analysis of the structure of the SYLLABLE, the term rhyme is used to refer to the nucleus and the coda together.

rhythm (50–51, 52, 54, 69) The feeling of movement in speech, based on the number of SYLLABLES, their timing, and STRESS.

schwa (18, 25) (Can also be spelled 'shwa') To make this VOWEL the lips are neither spread nor rounded, and the tongue is neither pushed forward or pulled back, nor raised nor lowered. Therefore, this vowel has a 'neutral' position, which is another term that can be used.

stress (51, 67, 69, 70, 71–2, 139) The property by means of which SYLLABLES are made to stand out from the other syllables in the stream of speech. If a syllable is produced with one or more of the following features, it will usually be perceived as being 'stressed': greater volume, length of vowel, higher or changing pitch than surrounding syllables.

stress-timing (52, 54) A type of RHYTHM in which the STRESSED SYLLABLES seem to occur at approximately regular intervals in time, and which typically involves compression and reduction in unstressed syllables. The other end of the continuum of types of rhythm in languages is referred to as 'syllable-timing', where the timing is based on the SYLLABLE.

syllable (52) The smallest unit of speech which normally occurs in isolation. A syllable can consist of a vowel, as in the word 'I' or a combination of vowel and consonant.

tone group (94–5) An intonational phrase. A group of syllables which have a movement in pitch used in the description and analysis of INTONATION (also referred to as a tone unit).

trill (36, 133) An articulation in which one articulator is held rather loosely against another so that the flow of air from the lungs causes one to flap a few times against the other, making a trilling sound.

velar (12, 27) A speech sound made with the back of the tongue in contact with or close to the VELUM or **soft palate**.

velum (3, 12) The soft muscular region of the roof of the mouth, also known as the 'soft palate'. This muscle can act like a flap or 'trap door' – when in a relaxed state, it allows air from the lungs to flow into the nasal cavity; or, it can be lifted up, thus 'closing the door' and preventing air from flowing into the nasal cavity.

weak form (81, 89) The usual, unstressed forms of words which contribute to the grammatical meaning of an utterance, e.g. articles, pronouns, prepositions, etc.

weak vowel (52, 54, 77, 81, 89, 139) A vowel that can only occur in unstressed SYLLABLES, not in syllables which receive STRESS. In English the most common weak vowels are /ə/ and /ɪ/.

word stress (70, 71–2) A fixed pattern of stressed or unstressed SYLLABLES within a word.

vocal cords (2) The flaps in the larynx which can open and close rapidly producing a vibrating noise known as VOICE.

voice (2, 40) In phonetics, the buzzing sound produced by the vibration of the vocal cords in the larynx.

vowel (1, 17–18) A speech sound which typically has voicing and no obstruction or audible friction in the vocal tract. In terms of the structure of a SYLLABLE, they comprise the essential part of the syllable, functioning as its core or 'nucleus'.

Further reading and references

The references in the Key and Comments sections are to the fifth edition of *Gimson's Pronunciation of English*, revised by A. Cruttenden. London: Edward Arnold, 1994.

Recent pronouncing dictionaries are:

Roach, P. and Hartmann, J. (eds) 1996: *English pronouncing dictionary*, 15th edn. Cambridge: Cambridge University Press.

Wells, J. C. (ed.) 1990: *Longman pronouncing dictionary*. Harlow: Longman.

Some recent books which are designed for teachers of English as an additional language are:

Brown, A. (ed.) 1991: *Teaching English pronunciation: a book of readings*. London and New York: Routledge.

Dalton, C. and Seidlhofer, B. 1994: *Pronunciation*. Oxford: Oxford University Press.

(This is an elegantly structured and comprehensive discussion of key aspects of teaching and learning the pronunciation of English.)

Gilbert, J. B. 1993: *Clear speech: pronunciation and listening comprehension in American English: teacher's resource book*, 2nd edn. Cambridge: Cambridge University Press.

A specialist periodical on English pronunciation teaching is:

Speak Out! The journal of the International Association of Teachers of English as a Foreign Language PronSIG (Pronunciation Special Interest Group) available from IATEFL, 3 Kingsdown Chambers, Kingsdown Park, Whitstable, Kent CT5 2DJ, England.

There are two course books for learners of English which provide accessible and clear presentations of the role of intonation in conveying meaning:

Bradford, B. 1988: *Intonation in context*. Cambridge: Cambridge University Press.

Brazil, D. 1994: *Pronunciation for advanced learners of English*. Cambridge: Cambridge University Press.

For general introductions to phonetics and phonology see:

Brown, G. 1990: *Listening to spoken English*, 2nd edn. Harlow: Longman.

(As well as an overview of aspects of sounds, rhythm and intonation, there is a chapter on paralinguistic features in this highly readable classic.)

Clark, J. and Yallop, C. 1995: *An introduction to phonetics and phonology*. Oxford: Blackwell.

Davenport, M. and Hannahs, S. J. 1998: *Introducing phonetics and phonology*. London: Arnold.

(In this book, Chapters 1–4 are useful as an overview; in later chapters Davenport and Hannahs discuss theoretical issues in phonological analysis in some detail.)

Katamba, F. 1989: *An introduction to phonology*. Harlow: Longman.

Kreidler, C. W. 1997: *Describing spoken English: an introduction*. London and New York: Routledge.

Ladefoged, P. 1993: *A course in phonetics*, 3rd edn. Fort Worth: Harcourt Brace College Publishers.

Laver, J. 1994: *Principles of phonetics*. Cambridge: Cambridge University Press.

Roach, P. 1991: *English phonetics and phonology: a practical course*, 2nd edn. Cambridge: Cambridge University Press.

(This gives a lucid introduction to all aspects of the sound system of British English, and includes exercises and tapes of examples.)

For the study of the accents of English see:

Hughes, A. and Trudgill, P. 1996: *English accents and dialects: an introduction to the social and regional varieties of English in the British Isles*, 2nd edn. London: Arnold.

Trudgill, P. and Hannah, J. 1982: *International English: a guide to the varieties of Standard English*, 3rd edn. London: Edward Arnold.

Wells, J. C. 1982: *Accents of English*, Volumes 1–3. Cambridge: Cambridge University Press.

(The accompanying tapes of the first two of these books give samples of a wide range of accents.)

For the area of intonation see:

Bolinger, D. 1989: *Intonation and its uses: melody in grammar and discourse*. London: Edward Arnold.

Cruttenden, A. 1986: *Intonation*. Cambridge: Cambridge University Press.

Tench, P. 1996: *The intonation systems of English*. London: Cassell.

For a discussion of the intonation patterns discussed in Unit 11 see:

Bradford, B. 1997. Upspeak in British English. *English Today* 51, **13**(3) (July), 29–36.

Britain, D. 1992. 'Linguistic change in intonation: the use of high rising terminals in New Zealand English. *Language Variation and Change* **4**(3), 77–105.

The following have useful and concise entries on many aspects of phonetics:

Crystal, D. 1995: *The Cambridge encyclopedia of language*. Cambridge: Cambridge University Press.

McArthur, T. (ed.) 1992: *The Oxford Companion to the English Language*. Oxford: Oxford University Press.

There are several introductory books on linguistics which have chapters on phonetics:

Cook, V. 1997: *Inside Language*. London: Arnold, 50–86.

(Cook gives a brief survey of /h/-dropping on pages 185–8.)

Graddol, D., Cheshire, J. and Swann, J. 1994: *Describing language*, 2nd edn. Buckingham: Open University Press.

Kuiper, K. and Allan, W. S. 1996: *An introduction to English language: sound, word and sentence*. Houndmills: Macmillan Press.

A brief introduction to pronunciation change is given in:

Trask, R. L. 1994: *Language change*. London: Routledge, 25–30.

More detailed accounts of the processes of phonetic and phonological change can be found in:

Smith, J. 1996: *An historical study of English: function, form and change*. London: Routledge, 79–111.

Trask, R. L. 1996: *Historical linguistics*. London: Arnold, 52–71.

(On pages 300–7 Trask discusses the processes of /h/-dropping and rhoticity and non-rhoticity in the history of English.)

For an overall survey of the history of the English Language, see:

Barber, C. 1993: *The English language: a historical introduction*. Cambridge: Cambridge University Press.

Baugh, A. C. and Cable, T. 1993: *A history of the English language*, 4th edn. London: Routledge.

The following book was used as the source for the Old English texts, and provides an introduction to the study of these manuscripts:

Wrenn, C. L. 1967: *A study of Old English literature*. New York: W.W. Norton.

A brief outline of the patterns of verse and metrical analysis can be found in:

Freeborn, D. with French, P. and Langford, D. 1993: *Varieties of English*, 2nd edn. Basingstoke: Macmillan Press.

A practical introduction to the way speech sounds and spellings map onto each other in English is:

Carney, E. 1997: *English spelling*. London: Routledge.

For a brief survey of the way children acquire the pronunciation of their first language see:
Foster, S. 1990: *The communicative competence of young children*. London: Longman, 44–8.

For a more detailed account of children's acquisition of English pronunciation, see:
Ingram, D. 1986: Phonological development: production. In Fletcher, P. and Garman, M. (eds). *Language acquisition*, 2nd edn. Cambridge: Cambridge University Press, 223–34.

In the same volume, there is an account of the child's development of stress and intonation:
Crystal, D. 1986: Prosodic Development. Ibid., 174–97.
Trudgill, P. 1974: *The social differentiation of English in Norwich*. Cambridge: Cambridge University Press.
Widdowson, H. G. 1992: *Practical stylistics*. Oxford: Oxford University Press.

The works of fiction referred to in the units are as follows:
Banks, I. 1992: *The Crow Road*. London: Abacus.
Doyle, A. C. 1995: *The Lost World and the Poison Belt*. Phoenix Mill: Alan Sutton.
MacDonald, G. 1964: *The Princess and the Goblin*. London: Puffin.
McEwan, I. 1998: *Enduring love*. London: Vintage.